— MY—
Grain & Brain
Cookbook

—MY—
Grain & Brain
Cookbook

101 Brain Healthy and Grain-free Recipes Everyone Can Use
To Boost Brain Power, Lose Belly Fat and Live Healthy

SHERYL JENSEN

Holison Press

Contact the author
shjensen@weightlosspeeps.com

ISBN-13: 978-1495320446
ISBN-10: 1495320448

Printed in the United States of America

Table of Contents

DISCLAIMER

The information provided in this book is for educational purposes only. I am not a physician and this is not to be taken as medical advice or a recommendation to stop eating other foods. This book is based on my experiences and interpretations of the past and current research available. If you have any health issues or pre-existing conditions, please consult your doctor before implementing any of the information that is presented in this book. Results may vary from individual to individual. This book is for informational purposes only and the author does not accept any responsibilities for any liabilities or damages, real or perceived, resulting from the use of this information.

STAY SMART, SLIM AND HEALTHY!

"Improve your brain health, lose weight and optimize your overall health – that's what you'll get from the gluten-free recipes in My Grain & Brain Cookbook"

Gluten consumption has justifiably become increasingly popular over the last decades. And no wonder – gluten, *the unhealthy protein component that is found in processed wheat and other grains* is available in an alarming variety of processed foods and even medications.

The health benefits of living without gluten are increasingly becoming widely acknowledged by scientists and doctors alike. Based on much scientific and medical evidence, life without gluten has many potential benefits, such as:

- Improved brain health
- Weight loss
- Improvement in gastrointestinal problems
- Increased energy
- Reduced bloating and gas
- Decreased risk of heart disease
- Improvement in allergy control
- Decreased cancer risk
- Improvement in symptoms of Celiac disease
- Reduced risk or improvement in of diabetes
- Plus improvement in overall healthy

Gluten Free Living Just Got Easier

Sadly, many people have misconceptions about going gluten-free, believing it is difficult to prepare and cook gluten-free. This is not entirely true, going gluten-free can be a stressful task, especially for beginners, but sometimes even for those who are already living the gluten-free lifestyle. However, it can become surprisingly simple if you follow the instructions given in the following pages. So, whether you are a total gluten-free newbie or not, your gluten-free journey can be so much easier with *My Brain & Grain Cookbook.*

My Brain & Grain Cookbook consists of 101 specially created, healthy and tasty gluten-free recipes. Apart from being gluten-free, these recipes are also wheat-free, low sugar, low carb and peanut-free. The choice of ingredients used in these recipes is carefully chosen, based on concrete scientific and medical research for a healthy gluten-free diet. Consequently, only the healthiest proteins, fats, fruits and vegetables are used in this book in order to ensure that you're eating to get the healthiest advantage.

So whether it's chicken kabobs or chocolate pudding, you'll surely find a healthy and strictly gluten-free recipe in *My Grain & Brain Cookbook.*

Who Can Use These Recipes?

Broadly speaking, these recipes are for everyone who wants to eat brain healthy foods, lose weight and live a healthy life. Even more specifically, these recipes are for you if you are looking for:

- Grain-free Recipes
- Brain Health Recipes
- Wheat-free Recipes
- Immune System Boosting Recipes
- Celiac-friendly Recipes
- Autoimmune-friendly Recipes
- Diabetic-friendly Recipes
- Low Sugar Recipes
- Protein-rich Recipes
- Low Carb Recipes
- Soy-free Recipes
- Peanut-free Recipes

THE GRAIN BLAME REALITY

Let's back track a bit. The truth is that we've been taught the wrong stuff about gluten over the decades. It all started centuries ago with the Egyptians. The Egyptians were the ones who started to store grains and use it as a contingency plan for times of drought and famine. In the interim, the use of non-genetically modified wheat in those challenging times had saved a lot of lives. From here, manufacturers of processed wheat and grains jumped on the bandwagon and we've been experiencing the distress of gluten ever since.

What Makes Gluten A Problem?

Simply put, there is a protein that is in grains such as wheat, oat, barley and rye. This protein is commonly mentioned as gluten. Now, this complex gluten protein is very difficult for our stomachs to digest. These difficult to digest complex protein will remain undigested in the body and triggers a host of other problems in the process. Of course, these digestive problems will have a negative impact on our health and trigger tissue destruction related intestinal problems such as Celiac Disease, Collitis, Irritable Bowel Syndrome, Chron's Disease and other chronic diseases. Furthermore, gluten sensitivity adversely affects our tissues and nervous system and is not always an intestinal problem. Consequently, cases of gluten sensitivity often go on to produce neurological symptoms.

Grain and Brain

For some time, the terms "grain" and "brain" have been widely used to refer to the correlation between grain consumption and brain health.

Today, statistical data have confirmed that there has been a significant increase of neurological disorders such as mild as brain fog or as severe as Alzheimer's disease, childhood development disorders, Parkinson's, autism, dementia, multiple sclerosis and other brain related neurogenerative disorders. As a result, various laboratory studies have been conducted to assist in identifying the cause of such a significant surge.

Increasingly, different laboratory findings have already confirmed that by eliminating gluten from the diet there has been an overwhelmingly positive effect on the brain health of many people. In fact, even a recent analysis study that was conducted by well-known immunologist, Aristo Vojdani, PhD based on blood samples from 400 healthy people, has revealed that there is a substantial connection between gluten consumption and neurological autoimmunity or reaction.

Based on the adverse reactions of gluten in the body, there is some form of "tagging" going on in the immune system in order to destroy complex gluten molecules. However, according to studies by immunologist, Aristo Vojdani, PhD and others, as in a case of mistaken identity, the immune system mistakably attacks and also destroys brain and nerve tissue while discerning that it is attacking the gluten. So in order words, gluten consumption is causing your immune system to mistakenly attack and destroy your brain.

Consider that if you've done tests that reveal that you're gluten sensitive you should adapt a gluten-free diet as quickly as possible. However, also bear in mind, that based on current gluten sensitivity tests, your sensitivity to gluten could go undetected for several years, even though gluten could still be negatively affecting your health.

So whether you've been diagnosed with gluten sensitivities or not, you should avoid gluten at all cost. Besides, many people who have adapted a gluten-free lifestyle have reported significant weight loss results and an overall improvement in their health. Save your brain and your health — go gluten-free!

GLUTEN-FREE FOR BEGINNERS

If you're already familiar with living gluten-free you may skip this section and go right into the healthy gluten-free recipes. However, if you are new to the gluten-free lifestyle, you may find this section to be quite useful.

Gluten-free Shopping

You're advised to go shopping before you start your exciting gluten-free lifestyle. Consider that preparation is essentially worth the effort and will make things so much easier. This will avoid you winding up in a frustrating situation where you are left with little or no options. Besides, lack of planning is the main reason for failures in life.

Before you go shopping, you can make a note of ingredients in the recipes that you will be preparing for a week or so. Your shopping list should be primarily based on the ingredients in the recipes. You should carefully create a shopping list before you head to the food store. Apart from the specific ingredients of the recipes, your list should always include ingredient extras and snacks. Please take a look at the 14 foods list guide in this book.

You will also need to clear your kitchen cabinets and refrigerator of the items that are not a part of the gluten-free diet or items that will not positively contribute to your gluten-free lifestyle goals. In doing so, you will need to get rid of bad fats, carbs, sugars so that you won't accidentally add them to a recipe or even feel tempted to use them.

Choosing your Food

Whenever you go gluten-free shopping you should ensure that you buy antibiotic-free and hormone-free animal, poultry, fish and red meat. You should look for free-range poultry and eggs as well as grass-fed beef, organic pork, wild fish or grass-fed butter. It is also important to choose freshly frozen meat which is also referred to as "flash" frozen.

You must also exercise caution when buying fruits, vegetables and nuts. Make an effort to buy fresh seasonal local vegetables and fruits that are certified to be organic. If you decide to get frozen fruits, you should ensure that they are free from added sugar. On the other hand, nuts should be raw and organic—most are welcome EXCEPT peanuts. Peanuts can be potentially harmful due to their ability to pull essential minerals away from the body. Pecans, walnuts, and almonds are great for snacking.

Though organic food is generally more expensive, the benefits far outweigh the cost. Organic food contains lower levels of pesticides, hormones, and antibiotics than conventional foods. Furthermore, studies have also revealed that organic foods also have more nutrients when compared to foods grown conventionally.

Essential Gluten-free Kitchen Tools

There are several essential tools that could make your gluten-free lifestyle much easier. Though not all of these items are needed for the recipes in this book, they are simply essential items that you'll find useful in your gluten-free kitchen.

Here is a list of some common essential gluten-free kitchen tools:
- A food processor
- A ladle
- A colander
- Ziplock storage bags of different sizes
- A powerful blender
- A slow cooker
- A dutch oven
- A grill pan
- A set of good-quality knives
- Wooden cutting boards—use separate boards for animal

products and fruits or vegetables
- An 8-inch nonstick sauté pan
- A 12-inch nonstick sauté pan (avoid non-stick pans with Teflon or other health risks due to poorer quality)
- An 8-quart stockpot
- Cooling rack
- 3 or 4 cookie or baking sheets
- Oven mittens
- Storage glass jars for condiments
- Natural parchment paper
- A lemon/citrus reamer
- A food mill/potato ricer
- A 2-quart saucepan with lid
- A 4-quart saucepan with lid
- A foil lined baking tray
- A coffee grinder for flaxseed or similar stuff
- Wire whisks
- Spring tongs
- Rubber spatulas
- Assorted measuring cups and spoons (1 quart, pint, 1 cup etc.) dry and liquid style
- A food scale
- Muffin pans
- Baking pans
- Skewers
- An instant-reac chef's thermometer
- Timer
- Mixing bowls of different sizes
- Electric mixer

Consider that this is not a conclusive list. Besides, you may already have some of these items in your kitchen.

LET'S GET STARTED

In *My Grain and Brain Cookbook,* you'll be able to take hold of healthy and mouthwatering gluten-free foods that will restore your brain and overall health and help you to take hold of your birthright to live a long and healthy life.

Whatever you choose from this special collection of over 100 gluten-free recipes, it's totally up to you. Just follow the instructions in this book and the different methods of preparing and cooking gluten-free will become surprisingly simple. In some cases, feel free to make your own gluten-free ingredient substitutions and tweak the recipes here and there based on your preferences or individual situations.

I have spent a lot of time to bring these recipes to perfection, but sometimes it's impossible to catch it all. So, if you see any glaring errors made in this book, please send me an email at shjensen@weightlosspeeps.com. I will be very grateful for your feedback.

Now, it's time to try your hand at creating healthy, easy and tasty gluten-free meals using these specially developed recipes.

Let us get into the recipes!

BREAKFASTS

Chicken Veggie Hash

This hearty dish has healthy proteins and healthy brain boosting fats. The medley of chicken and vegetables is also a tasty pleaser.

Serves: 4
Prep Time: 10 minutes
Cooking Time: 20 minutes

1½ teaspoons extra-virgin coconut oil
2 cloves garlic, chopped
2-3 turnips, peeled and chopped into cubes
¼ cup onion, chopped
1 medium tomato, chopped
½ cup red bell pepper, seeded and chopped
½ cup cooked grass-fed chicken, chopped
½ cup spinach, trimmed and torn
Flaked sea salt and black pepper, to taste

Directions

1. In a non-stick pan, heat oil on medium heat.
2. Add onion and sauté for about 1 minute.
3. Add turnip and cook stirring often for about 5 minutes.
4. Add onion, tomato and bell pepper and cook, stirring often for 5 minutes.
5. Add chicken and cook for 4 to 5 minutes.
6. Add spinach and cook for 2 to 3 minutes or until just wilted.
7. Season with salt and black pepper.
8. Serve this hash with poached eggs.

Crunchy Almond Pancakes

These golden and fluffy pancakes make a perfectly superb weekend breakfast. The recipe of these pancakes offers a naturally healthy gluten-free version of regular pancakes.

Serves: *4*
Prep Time: *10 minutes*
Cooking Time: *20 minutes*

½ cup coconut flour
½ cup almond flour
½ teaspoon non-aluminum baking soda
½ cup almond milk
¼ cup almond butter, melted
4 free-range eggs, beaten
1 teaspoon fresh lemon juice
1 tablespoon natural stevia
¼ cup almonds, chopped
Extra-virgin coconut oil, for cooking

Directions

1. In a bowl, add flours and baking soda and mix well.
2. In another bowl, add butter and milk and beat well.
3. Add eggs, lemon juice and stevia and beat until well combined.
4. Mix egg mixture into flour mixture.
5. Fold in chopped almonds.
6. In a large frying pan, heat oil on medium heat.
7. Add mixture in desired size.
8. Cook for 3 to 4 minutes per side.

9. Repeat with the remaining mixture.
10. Serve with almond butter.

Mini Kale & Mushrooms Quiches

These quiches are interesting to add to your breakfast menu or even for brunch. Sautéed kale and mushrooms keep these mini quiches savory and yummy.

Serves: *2*
Prep Time: *10 minutes*
Cooking Time: *22 minutes*

---

1 teaspoon extra-virgin olive oil
½ cup mushroom, sliced
1 cup kale, trimmed and torn
2 free-range eggs
½ teaspoon dried rosemary, crushed
Flaked sea salt and black pepper, to taste
½ cup parmesan cheese, grated
½ tablespoon unsweetened coconut cream or coconut milk

Directions

1. Preheat the oven to 375 degrees F.
2. Lightly, grease a 6 cups muffins tray.
3. In a pan, heat oil on medium heat.
4. Add mushrooms and sauté for about 4 to 5 minutes.
5. Transfer the mushrooms in a plate.
6. In the same pan, add kale and sauté for 3 to 4 minutes or until just wilted. Take from heat.
7. In a bowl, add eggs, rosemary, salt and black pepper and beat well.
8. Add mushrooms, kale, cheese and cream in egg mixture and mix until well combined.

9. Place the mixture in prepared muffins tray.
10. Bake for 20 to 22 minutes or until a toothpick inserted in the center comes out clean.
11. Serve these quiches with fresh greens.

Mushroom Artichoke Frittata

Try a hearty frittata that is also excellent for breakfast or brunch. You'll enjoy the amazing texture and taste of this frittata.

Serves: *2*
Prep Time: *10 minutes*
Cooking Time: *25 minutes*

---

1 tablespoon of extra-virgin coconut oil, divided
2 baby artichokes, trimmed and halved
Flakes sea salt and black pepper, to taste
1/3 cup water
1 small clove garlic, chopped finely
2 medium free-range eggs
1½ tablespoons feta cheese, crumbled
1½-ounces (about 2 tablespoons) mushrooms, sliced thinly

Directions

1. In a pan, heat 1 tablespoon of oil on medium-high heat.
2. Add artichokes. Sprinkle a pinch of salt and black pepper. Sauté for about 3 to 4 minutes.
3. Reduce the heat to medium-low. Add water and garlic. Cover and simmer for about 10 minutes. Uncover and cook until all water is absorbed. Remove from stove. Pat dry the artichokes with a paper towel. Leave any excess oil in the skillet.
4. Preheat the broiler.
5. In a bowl, add eggs, ½ tablespoon of cheese and pinch of salt and black pepper and beat until well

combined.

6. In an oven-proof skillet, heat remaining oil (or add ½ tablespoon coconut oil if necessary) on medium-high heat. Add mushrooms and sauté for about 3 to 4 minutes or until brown.

7. Add sautéed artichokes and continue to cook, stirring for about 2 minutes.

8. Stir in eggs. Reduce the heat to medium. Cover and cook for about 3 to 4 minutes or until eggs are set.

9. Sprinkle remaining cheese on top.

10. Now, place the skillet in broiler. Broil for about 1 minute.

11. Serve this frittata with green salad.

Cheesy Pepper Baked Eggs

This recipe is very easy and has very little hassle. These baked eggs with roasted peppers and cheese makes a healthy meal for breakfast.

Serves: *4*
Prep Time: *5 minutes*
Cooking Time: *15 minutes*

¼ cup roasted green peppers, chopped finely
¼ cup roasted red peppers, chopped finely
8 free-range eggs
4 teaspoons mozzarella cheese, grated freshly

Directions

1. Preheat the oven to 350 degrees F.
2. In a large baking dish, spread both peppers evenly.
3. Crack the eggs and place over peppers.
4. Sprinkle cheese over eggs evenly.
5. Bake for about 15 minutes or until eggs are completely set.
6. Serve these baked eggs with gluten-free quinoa bread slices or avocado slices.

Cinnamon Pumpkin Bread

This classic and moist bread has the rich aroma of cinnamon. This cinnamon pumpkin bread actually tastes even better the day after it has been baked.

Serves: *4*
Prep Time: *10 minutes*
Cooking Time: *45 minutes*

---

1 cup almond flour
½ teaspoon non-aluminum baking soda
1 tablespoon cinnamon powder
¼ teaspoon flaked sea salt
1 teaspoon gluten-free pumpkin pie spice
3 large range free eggs, beaten
½ cup pumpkin, roasted and mashed
1 tablespoon natural stevia

Directions

1. Preheat the oven to 350 degrees F.
2. Grease a loaf pan.
3. In a bowl, add flour, baking soda, cinnamon, salt and pumpkin pie spice and mix well.
4. In another bowl, add eggs, pumpkin and stevia and beat until well mixed.
5. Mix flour mixture into egg mixture.
6. Place the pumpkin mixture in prepared loaf pan.
7. Bake for about 35 to 45 minutes.

Spinach & Green Peppers Omelet

This recipe is perfect for spinach lovers or those who want to mix their spinach with eggs. This omelet is also a great source of vitamin D and protein.

Serves: *2*
Prep Time: *5 minutes*
Cooking Time: *5 minutes*

---

3 teaspoons extra-virgin coconut oil, divided
½ cup green bell pepper, seeded, roasted, remove seeds and black skin and cut into thin strips
¾ cup spinach, stemmed and torn
Flaked sea salt, to taste
Black pepper powder, to taste
Cayenne pepper, to taste
2 tablespoons water
4 free-range eggs
2 tablespoons parmesan cheese, shredded

Directions

1. In a non-stick frying pan, add 2 teaspoons of oil and bell pepper and just heat for about 1 minute.
2. Add spinach and cook until just wilted for about 30 to 40 seconds.
3. Remove from pan and transfer into a bowl. Sprinkle a tiny pinch of salt, black pepper and cayenne pepper.
4. In another bowl, add water, eggs, pinch of salt and black pepper and beat until well combined.

5. Coat a non-stick frying pan with remaining oil. Heat the pan on medium heat.
6. Add the beaten eggs in pan and reduce the heat to medium-low.
7. Cook, without stirring for about 2 minutes.
8. Place the spinach mixture in the center. Sprinkle the cheese over spinach mixture.
9. Then roll the omelet and place into a serving plate.
10. Serve this omelet with avocado slices.

Vanilla Pear Fritters

These yummy fritters are excellent for a protein-rich and fruity breakfast. This is a kid's favorite, so don't be surprised if your kids ask for more.

Serves: 2
Prep Time: 10 minutes
Cooking Time: 5 minutes

½ tablespoon of flaxseed powder
6 tablespoons almond meal, powdered finely
¼ cup arrowroot starch
¼ teaspoon non-aluminum baking soda
¼ teaspoon flaked sea salt
1 small free-range egg
2 tablespoons unsweetened almond milk
¼ teaspoon apple cider vinegar
½ tablespoon natural stevia
½ teaspoon gluten-free vanilla extract
1 pear, peeled, cored and cut into 1/3-inch slices
Coconut oil, for frying

Directions

1. In a bowl, add flaxseed, almond meal, arrowroot starch, baking soda and salt and mix well.
2. In another bowl, add egg, almond milk, apple cider, stevia and vanilla and beat until well combined.
3. Mix flour mixture into egg mixture.
4. In a pan, heat oil on medium heat.
5. Coat sliced pear in the mixture.

6. Add pear slices in pan and cook for about 2 minutes from both sides.
7. Serve these fritters with the dusting of cinnamon powder.

Veggie Breakfast Scramble

This veggie delight makes a yummy and satisfying breakfast. Plus, this is a scramble that is packed with rich antioxidants and protein.

Serves: *2*
Prep Time: *5 minutes*
Cooking Time: *5 minutes*

---

3 teaspoons extra-virgin coconut oil
½ green bell pepper, seeded and chopped
½ cup kale, trimmed and chopped finely
½ tomato, seeded and chopped finely
2 free-range eggs, beaten lightly
Flaked sea salt and black pepper, to taste
Pinch of paprika

Directions

1. In a nonstick pan, add oil and heat on medium heat.
2. Add vegetables and cook for about 2 to 3 minutes.
3. Add eggs and cook, stirring continuously for about 1 to 2 minutes.
4. Season with salt, black pepper and paprika.
5. This is optional, but you may top this scramble with chopped scallions before serving.

Wholesome Coconut Porridge

Enjoy this wholesome fruity coconut porridge and stay fully energized for hours. This mouthful of goodness is a sure way to feed your brain in the morning. Remember that this meal should be used in moderation due to the sweetness of the ripe banana.

Serves: *4*
Prep Time: *10 minutes*
Cooking Time: *15 minutes*

---

8 free-range eggs, beaten
1 medium ripe banana, mashed
2 tablespoons coconut flakes, shredded
1/3 cup unsweetened coconut milk
2 tablespoons natural almond butter
½ teaspoon organic vanilla powder
1½ cups apples, peeled, cored and chopped

Directions

1. In a large bowl, add all ingredients except apple and beat until well combined.
2. Ad apple and mix.
3. In a non-stick pan, add fruit mixture on medium heat.
4. Cook, stirring frequently for about 10 to 15 minutes or until a thick porridge forms.
5. Top with maraschino cherries.

Pumpkin Pancakes

These pancakes are delicious and are perfect for a holiday or weekend breakfast. Enjoy them anytime you wish.

Serves: 2
Prep Time: 10 minutes
Cooking Time: 10 minutes

---

1 cup coconut flour
½ teaspoon non-aluminum baking soda
½ teaspoon non-aluminum, gluten free baking powder
½ teaspoon gluten-free pumpkin pie spice
1 cup unsweetened almond milk
1 free-range egg
1 tablespoon organic coconut butter, melted
Coconut oil, for cooking

Directions

1. In a bowl, add flour, baking soda, baking powder and all spice powder and mix well.
2. In another bowl, add almond milk, egg and butter and beat until well combined.
3. Mix egg mixture into flour mixture.
4. Coat a non-stick pan with coconut oil and heat on medium heat.
5. In heated pan, place the mixture according to the size you like.
6. Cook for 3 to 4 minutes per side.
7. Enjoy these pancakes with fresh fruit of your choice (make sure to use fruits that are less sweet).

Chocolate Coconut Squares

This wonderfully protein-rich recipe provides lots of energy. Enjoy this treat for breakfast or even dessert if you please.

Serves: *2*
Prep Time: *5 minutes*
Cooking Time: *2 minutes plus setting time in the refrigerator*

¼ cup almond butter
¼ cup gluten-free cocoa powder
Natural stevia, to taste
¼ cup almond meal, grounded finely
1/3 cup sunflower seeds
1/3 cup pumpkin seeds
1 cup unsweetened coconut flakes, shredded
1 teaspoon almond extract
Pinch of flaked sea salt

Directions

1. Lightly, grease a baking dish.
2. In a pan, beat together butter, cocoa powder and stevia.
3. Bring to a boil, stirring often for about 1 minute.
4. Remove from heat and immediately stir in remaining ingredients.
5. Place the seed mixture in prepared dish.
6. Let it cool at room temperature.
7. Refrigerate to set completely.
8. When it hardens, cut into squares.

9. Serve these healthy bars with the topping of 70 % or more dark chocolate shaving.

Turnip Tortillas

These tortillas are a classic hit over traditional tortillas but really soft and tasty. Try these tortillas for a warm and healthy meal.

Serves: *4*
Prep Time: *10 minutes*
Cooking Time: *60 minutes*

½ pound (226 grams) turnip, peeled and sliced
1 teaspoon extra-virgin coconut oil
1 clove garlic, minced
Flaked sea salt and black pepper, to taste
4 large free-range eggs
1 large free-range egg white
1 tablespoon chives, chopped and divided
1½ tablespoons parmesan cheese, grated

Directions

1. Preheat the oven to 350 degrees F.
2. In a water filled pan, add turnip. Bring to boil on medium heat.
3. Reduce heat to medium-low. Simmer for about 25 minutes or until tender.
4. Drain and let it cool.
5. In an oven proof non-stick skillet, melt coconut oil on medium heat.
6. Add turnip and garlic and sauté for about 30 to 40 seconds.
7. Sprinkle with pinch of salt and black pepper.
8. With a spatula, press turnip in the bottom of skillet.

9. In a bowl, add eggs, egg white, chives and pinch of salt and black pepper and beat until well combined.
10. Pour egg mixture on turnip and stir gently.
11. Cook for about 2 minutes.
12. Remove from heat and top with cheese.
13. Serve this dish with the topping of plum tomatoes.

Yummy Banana Muffins

These banana muffins are not only delicious, but they are completely gluten-free and brain healthy. Make a yummy breakfast with these muffins. Remember that this meal should be used in moderation due to the sweetness of the ripe banana.

Serves: 4
Prep Time: 5 minutes
Cooking Time: 5 minutes

½ cup coconut flour
½ cup almond flour
½ teaspoon non-aluminum baking soda
½ teaspoon cinnamon powder
Pinch of flaked sea salt
6 small free-range eggs
1 teaspoon gluten-free vanilla extract
Natural stevia, to taste
3 tablespoons coconut oil
3 ripe bananas, mashed

Directions

1. Preheat the oven to 350 degrees F. Grease a muffin pan.
2. In a large bowl, mix together flours, baking soda, cinnamon and salt
3. In another bowl, add remaining ingredients and beat until well combined.
4. Mix egg mixture into flour mixture. Add a little unsweetened almond milk if the mixture appears too

dry. It should not be a runny mixture.

5. Place the mixture in prepared muffin pan.
6. Bake for 20 to 25 minutes or until a toothpick inserted in the center comes out clean.

Crustless Mushroom Quiche

Try this sumptuous mushroom dish and top up your vitamin D (oh yes!) while you also boost your immune system and your overall health. This dish is perfect for breakfast or whenever you wish.

Serves 4
Preparation Time: 15 minutes
Cooking Time: 35 minutes

---

1 pound (453 grams) fresh mushroom
3 tablespoons chopped onion
3 free-range eggs, beaten
6 tablespoons grass-fed butter
½ teaspoon nutmeg
1 tablespoon arrowroot powder
1 teaspoon water (add more if needed)
Flaked sea salt to taste

Directions

1. In a large skillet, melt the butter. Sauté the onions until it becomes golden brown. Add in the mushrooms and nutmeg. Cook, while stirring occasionally, until the mushrooms become tender.
2. Preheat oven to 375 degrees Fahrenheit.
3. Make a paste with the arrowroot starch and water, and mix it into the mushroom mixture. Combine the salt with the beaten eggs and add it to the mushroom mixture also.
4. Pour the mixture into a greased oven-proof pie dish and bake in the preheated oven for 30 minutes or

until a skewer or toothpick inserted in the middle comes out clean.

Almond Ginger Cookies

These ginger cookies are nicely complete with a hint of ginger and will stay fresh for days. Enjoy the aroma while you bake them.

Serves: *4*
Prep Time: *10 minutes*
Cooking Time: *10 minutes*

---

1 cup almond flour
2 teaspoons non-aluminum baking soda
1 teaspoon cinnamon powder
1 tablespoon ground ginger
½ teaspoon flaked sea salt
1 free-range egg
¾ cup almond butter
1 tablespoon natural stevia
¼ cup no-sugar-added applesauce (homemade is best)

Directions

1. Preheat the oven to 350 degrees F.
2. In a bowl, add almond flour, baking powder, cinnamon, ginger and salt and mix well.
3. In another bowl, add remaining ingredients and beat until well combined.
4. Mix egg mixture into flour mixture.
5. Place the mixture on cookie sheet according to size of your choice.
6. Bake for 8 to 10 minutes.

Chocolate Nut Bars

Chocolate nut bars are great for a delicious and healthy breakfast. These bars give natural energy with the walnuts and chocolate combination.

Serves: *4*
Prep Time: *10 minutes*
Cooking Time: *25 minutes*

---

2 cups walnuts
2 free-range eggs
1 tablespoon organic cocoa powder
1 tablespoon gluten free vanilla extract
Pinch of flaked sea salt
½ cup dark chocolate chips (70% or more cocoa)
Natural stevia to taste (optional)

Directions

1. Preheat the oven to 350 degrees F.
2. Lightly, grease a baking dish.
3. In a food processor, add walnuts and pulse until a coarse meal forms.
4. Add eggs, cocoa, vanilla, stevia (if using) and salt and pulse until well combined.
5. Fold in chocolate chips.
6. Place the mixture in prepared baking dish.
7. Bake for 25 minutes.
8. Cool it and cut into desired size.
9. Serve with the topping of chopped walnuts.

Zesty Blueberry Bread

This bread is a special treat for a wonderful breakfast. Definitely, this moist bread will be a favorite for many and especially for lemon lovers.

Serves: *4*
Prep Time: *10 minutes*
Cooking Time: *4 minutes*

---

2 cups almond flour
1 teaspoon non-aluminum, gluten free baking powder
¼ teaspoon cinnamon powder
1 teaspoon flaked sea salt
½ cup coconut oil, melted
2 tablespoons natural stevia
2 free-range eggs
1 teaspoon fresh lemon juice
¼ cup blueberries
2 teaspoons lemon zest, grated freshly

Directions

1. Preheat the oven to 350 degrees F.
2. Lightly, grease a loaf pan.
3. In a bowl, add flour, baking powder, cinnamon and salt and mix well.
4. In another bowl, add oil, stevia and lemon juice and beat until well combined.
5. Mix egg mixture into flour mixture.
6. Fold in blueberries and lemon zest.
7. Bake for about 40 minutes or until a toothpick inserted in the center comes out clean.

SALADS & MEATLESS DISHES

Cheesy Summer Squash Casserole

This delicious summer squash recipe is balanced with proteins for optimal brain health benefits. In addition, this simple meal is packed with cancer-fighting and heart-protecting health benefits plus more.

Serves 4
Preparation Time: 15 minutes
Cooking Time: 30 minutes

2 pounds (453 grams) summer squash, ends trimmed and cut into ½ inch slices
2 tablespoons chopped fresh parsley
1 large onion
2 tablespoons extra-virgin olive oil
½ pound (226 grams) goat cheese
2 free-range eggs beaten
½ teaspoon freshly ground black pepper
Flaked sea salt to taste

Directions

1. In a large non-stick skillet, add the oil and onion and cook until the onion is soft.
2. Steam the summer squash in a metal steamer (or covered pot with water) on medium flame until the peel becomes soft or for about 3 minutes. Drain any excess liquid after steaming and arrange the squash at the bottom of a greased oven-proof casserole dish.
3. Crumble the goat cheese on top.
4. Preheat oven to 375 degrees Fahrenheit.
5. In a small bowl, add the parsley, eggs, salt and black pepper and stir well to combine. Pour this mixture over the cheese topped squash in the casserole dish.
6. Bake in a preheated oven for approximately 25 minutes. Serve warm or at room temperature.

Cauliflower Couscous with Walnuts

Cauliflower couscous pairs well with walnuts. Lime is also added to balance the rich nutty taste of this unique dish.

Serves: *4*
Prep Time: *10 minutes*
Cooking Time: *10 minutes*

---

1 large head of cauliflower, removed stems and chopped roughly
3 tablespoons extra-virgin coconut oil, divided
1 large yellow onion, chopped
Flaked sea salt, to taste
½ cup walnuts, toasted and chopped
¼ cup fresh cilantro, chopped
1 teaspoon fresh lime juice
1 teaspoon lime zest, grated freshly
Black pepper, to taste

Directions:

1. To make cauliflower couscous: in a food processor, add cauliflower and pulse until couscous consistency forms.
2. In a nonstick skillet, heat 2 tablespoons oil on medium-high heat.
3. Add onion and sauté for 4 to 5 minutes.
4. Add cauliflower couscous and some salt.
5. Cook, stirring for 4 to 5 minute.
6. Transfer the couscous in serving bowl.

7. Add remaining ingredients and mix well.
8. Top with chopped cherry tomatoes.

Baby Spinach Olive Salad

This salad is a classic combination of spinach, beets and olives. The flavors of this salad work very nicely together.

Servings: 2
Prep Time: 10 minutes
Cooking Time: 10 minutes

½ tablespoon extra-virgin coconut oil
½ cup red onion, sliced thinly
1 garlic clove, chopped finely
2 tablespoons kalamata olives, sliced thinly
½ cup beets, sliced thinly
1 tablespoon balsamic vinegar
Flaked sea salt and black pepper, to taste
4 cups baby spinach

Directions:

1. In a non-stick skillet, heat oil on medium heat.
2. Add onion and sauté for about 2 minutes or until soft.
3. Add garlic and olives and cook, stirring for about 2 to 3 minutes.
4. Add beets, vinegar, salt and pepper and cook for about 2 to 3 minutes.
5. Remove from heat.
6. In a large serving bowl, place baby spinach.
7. Add the beet mixture and toss to coat well.
8. Serve warm.

Cheesy Italian Broccoli Casserole

This cheesy broccoli casserole can please even the pickiest eaters. The dish requires little preparation time and results in a fulfilling meal.

Serves: *2*
Prep Time: *10 minutes*
Cooking Time: *10 minutes*

½ pound (226 grams) broccoli, cut into florets
1 tablespoon almond butter or organic pasture-fed butter, melted
Italian seasoning, to taste
Flaked sea salt and black pepper, to taste
¼ cup mozzarella cheese, grated

Directions

1. In a water-filled pan, add broccoli and bring to a boil.
2. Cover and cook for about 8 to 10 minutes.
3. Drain well.
4. Place broccoli in a microwave safe casserole dish.
5. Drizzle melted butter over broccoli.
6. Season with Italian seasoning, salt and black pepper.
7. Top with cheese.
8. Microwave on high for 1 minute. If you are a bit picky about the microwave, bake at 350 degrees Fahrenheit for about 4-5 minutes.
9. Serve with lime slices.

Lemony Almond Broccoli

Broccoli is a great vegetable for healthy nutrition. This is an easy and quick broccoli recipe with a delicious tangy flavor.

***Servings:** 2-3*
***Prep Time:** 10 minutes*
***Cooking Time:** 10 minutes*

---

1 broccoli head, cut into florets
¼ cup almond butter
¼ cup almonds, blanched, slivered and chopped
1 teaspoon lemon zest, grated freshly
2 tablespoons fresh lemon juice

Directions

1. In a water filled pan, add broccoli and cook on low heat for about 6 to 8 minutes. Drain well.
2. Meanwhile, in a pan, heat butter and remove from heat.
3. Add almonds, lemon zest and juice and stir well.
4. Place warm broccoli in serving bowl.
5. Pour lemon mixture over broccoli and serve immediately.

Gingery Summer Squash Soup with Apple

With its unique taste, this recipe makes an easy soup for any menu. Enjoy it for dinner or maybe even lunch.

Servings: *4*
Prep Time: *1 hour 10 minutes*
Cooking Time: *15 minutes*

---

2 tablespoons extra-virgin olive oil
3 small cloves garlic, chopped
1 small onion, chopped finely
2 tablespoons fresh ginger, grated freshly
½ teaspoon gluten-free pumpkin pie spice
½ teaspoon turmeric powder
3 cups low sodium gluten-free vegetable broth
5 cups summer squash, chopped
1 tart apple peeled, cored and chopped
Flaked sea salt and black pepper, to taste

Directions:

1. In a large soup pot, heat oil on medium heat.
2. Add garlic and onion and sauté for 4 to 5 minutes.
3. Add ginger and spices and sauté for 1 minute more.
4. Add broth, summer squash and apple and bring to a boil.
5. Reduce the heat to medium-low. Cover partially and simmer for about 20 to 25 minutes.
6. Remove from heat and let it cool.
7. In a blender, add soup and puree.

8. Transfer the soup in pot again. Season with salt and black pepper.
9. Heat completely before serving.
10. Serve this soup with the drizzling of a little fresh lemon juice.

Cilantro Chard Stew

This chard stew is a highly satisfying and tasty dish. Enjoy the nutritious antioxidant and omega fatty acid benefits of chard in this delicious stew.

Serves: *4*
Prep Time: *10 minutes*
Cooking Time: *20 minutes*

1½ tablespoons coconut or grass-fed butter, divided
3 garlic cloves, minced
Flaked sea salt and black pepper, to taste
1 tablespoon coriander powder
2 cups fresh cilantro, chopped roughly and divided
3 cups reduced sodium gluten-free vegetable broth
1½ pounds (680 grams) chard, removed ribs and cut the leaves in strips
½ of small red onion, chopped finely
½ tablespoon fresh lime juice
1 tablespoon balsamic vinegar

Directions

1. In a large pan, melt half of butter on medium-high heat.
2. Add garlic, salt, black pepper and coriander powder and cook, stirring for about 1 minute.
3. Add 1 cup of cilantro and cook for 1 minute more.
4. Add broth and bring to a boil.
5. Reduce the heat to medium. Simmer for about 10 minutes.

6. Add chard and cook for 4 to 5 minutes.
7. Meanwhile in a small pan, melt remaining butter on medium-high heat.
8. Add remaining cilantro and cook for 1 minute.
9. In a bowl, add onion, lime juice and vinegar and mix well.
10. While serving, add buttered cilantro and onion mixture in chard stew and mix well.

Herbed Tomato Soup

This tasty soup is a great way to make use of fresh tomatoes from the food store or your garden. Enjoy a bowl of powerful antioxidant goodness while also boosting your brain's health.

Serves: *4*
Prep Time: *10 minutes*
Cooking Time: *25 minutes*

---

3 large tomatoes, peeled and chopped finely
¼ cup fresh basil, chopped
1 small white onion, chopped finely
4 garlic cloves, minced
2 cups reduced sodium gluten-free chicken broth
Pinch of marjoram
¼ teaspoon oregano, crushed
¼ teaspoon dried thyme, crushed
Flaked sea salt and black pepper, to taste

Directions

1. In a large soup pan, add all ingredients.
2. Bring to a boil on medium-high heat.
3. Reduce the heat to medium-low.
4. Cover and simmer for 20 minutes. Let it cool.
5. In a blender, add soup and puree in batches until smooth.
6. Transfer the soup in pan again and heat completely.
7. Garnish this soup with fresh chopped basil leaves.

Egg & Cucumber Salad

This is a light but protein-rich meal. The crunchy vegetables add color, fiber and nutrients to this egg salad. This salad must be consumed with moderation due to the yogurt ingredient or feel free to make your own substitutions.

Serves: 4
Prep Time: 10 minutes

---

8 free-range eggs, hard boiled and chopped
½ cup cucumber, chopped
½ cup cabbage, chopped
¼ cup carrots, peeled and chopped finely
2 tablespoons scallions, sliced thinly
¼ cup non-fat plain yogurt
Flaked sea salt and black pepper

Directions

1. In a large serving bowl, add eggs and vegetables and gently mix.
2. In another bowl, add yogurt, salt and black pepper and mix well.
3. Add yogurt mixture into vegetables and gently mix.
4. Top this salad with chopped nuts.

Coconut Flavored Cauliflower Casserole

This cauliflower casserole is unbelievably delicious. The sauce is full of spicy garlic flavors which help to enhance the taste of the casserole. This dish must be consumed with moderation due to the carrot ingredient or feel free to make your own substitutions.

Serves: 4
Prep Time: 10 minutes
Cooking Time: 30 minutes

---

2 tablespoons extra-virgin coconut oil
1 onion, minced
2 clove garlic, minced
1¼ head cauliflower, chopped
1 carrot, grated

For Sauce:
1 cup coconut milk
2 tablespoons arrowroot starch
½ cup nutritional yeast
1 teaspoon raw coconut vinegar
1 teaspoon mustard powder
1 tablespoon coconut oil
½ teaspoon cayenne pepper
Flaked sea salt and black pepper, to taste

Directions:

1. Preheat the oven to 350 degrees F.
2. In a large pan heat oil on medium-low heat.

3. Add onion and garlic and sauté for 2 to 3 minutes.
4. Add chopped cauliflower and cook for 5 to 7 minutes.
5. Meanwhile, in a bowl, add all the sauce ingredients and beat until well combined.
6. In a casserole dish, place the vegetable mixture.
7. Stir in the sauce.
8. Bake for 15 to 20 minutes.
9. Serve his casserole with the topping of chopped almonds.

Buttery Spaghetti Squash with Fresh Herbs

This dish is delicious and simply cooked with butter and fresh herbs. Fresh herbs pairs well with the subtle flavors of the spaghetti squash. Great for a "go-easy" meal choice.

Serves: 4
Prep Time: 10 minutes
Cooking Time: 3 minutes

2½ tablespoons coconut butter or organic grass-fed butter
2 pounds (907 grams) spaghetti squash, roasted, peeled, seeded and scooped out the flesh
Flaked sea salt and black pepper, to taste
2 tablespoons fresh mixed herbs (chives, parsley, basil and sage), chopped finely

---

Directions

1. In a non-stick skillet, melt butter on medium heat.
2. Add all the remaining ingredients and cook for 2 to 3 minutes.
3. Serve with lime slices or avocado slices.

Apple & Fennel Soup

Here comes a comforting and savory recipe for dinner. Apple and fennel when combined in this dish adds a distinctive flavor in this healthy soup.

Serves: *4*
Prep Time: *10 minutes*
Cooking Time: *22 minutes*

---

2 tablespoons extra-virgin olive oil
1 onion, chopped
2 large apples, peeled, cored and sliced
2 large fennel bulbs, removed stems and sliced
2 cups gluten-free chicken broth
2 tablespoons fresh basil, chopped
Flaked sea salt and black pepper, to taste

Directions

1. In a large soup pan, heat oil on medium-low heat.
2. Add onion and sauté for 8 to 10 minutes.
3. Add apple and fennel and cook, stirring for about 8 to 10 minutes.
4. Add basil and chicken broth.
5. Cook for 2 minutes and let it cool slightly.
6. In a food processor, add soup and blend in batches until creamy and smooth.
7. Transfer the soup in pan again.
8. Heat the soup completely before serving
9. Top this soup with fresh coriander leaves and avocado slices.

Veggie Ratatouille

This fresh vegetable combination makes this dish not only flavorful, but also healthy. Enjoy this flavorful and nutritious veggie dish.

Serves: *4*
Prep Time: *20 minutes*
Cooking Time: *50 minutes*

¼ cup of extra-virgin coconut oil, divided
1 white onion, sliced thinly
2 garlic cloves, chopped
3 (green, yellow and red each) bell peppers, seeded and cubed
1 medium yellow squash, cubed
1 zucchini, cubed
1 bay leaf
1 tablespoon fresh thyme, chopped
1 tablespoon fresh oregano, chopped
2 plum tomatoes, chopped
Flaked sea salt and black pepper, to taste

Directions

1. In a large skillet, heat 1 teaspoon oil on medium-low heat.
2. Add onion and garlic and sauté for 4 to 5 minutes.
3. In another large skillet, add 1 tablespoon of oil and sauté bell peppers for 2 to 3 minutes.
4. Transfer the bell peppers in skillet of onion.
5. Sauté the remaining vegetables in batches, one at a time, adding required oil.

6. Transfer all vegetables in skillet of onion.
7. Add bay leaf, thyme and oregano.
8. Cover and cook for 15 to 20 minutes.
9. Now, add tomatoes and season with salt and pepper.
10. Cover and cook for 10 to 15 minutes.
11. Remove bay leaf and serve.
12. Serve this veggie ratatouille with the garnishing of chopped fresh coriander.

Buttery Brussels Sprout with Red Grapes

This great tasting recipe is a wonderful change from simple Brussels sprout. This earthy dish may be also perfect for holidays based on its festive colors.

Serves: 4
Prep Time: 10 minutes
Cooking Time: 35 minutes

---

2 pounds (907 grams) Brussels sprouts, trimmed
2 tablespoons extra-virgin coconut oil
2 bunches scallions, chopped
4 garlic cloves, minced
½ cup seedless red grapes, halved
3 tablespoons coconut butter or organic or pasture-fed butter

---

Directions

1. In a salted water filled pot, add Brussels sprout and bring to a boil.
2. Cook for about 10 minutes or until tender.
3. Meanwhile, in a pan, heat oil on medium-low heat.
4. Add scallions and garlic. Cook, stirring for about 5 minutes.
5. Add grapes, butter and Brussels sprouts.
6. Reduce the heat to medium. Cover and simmer for about 15 to 20 minutes.
7. Top with chopped fresh basil.

Roasted Summer Squash with Herbs

This interesting dish is colorful in appearance. Fresh herbs add earthy balance to the summer squash and the milky twist from the goat cheese makes this dish very tasty.

Serves: 4
Prep Time: 10 minutes
Cooking Time: 16 minutes

---

4 summer squashes, sliced into ½-inch thick pieces
½ teaspoon fresh oregano, chopped
½ teaspoon fresh thyme, chopped
½ teaspoon fresh rosemary, chopped
Flaked sea salt and black pepper, to taste
1 tablespoon extra-virgin olive oil
2 tablespoons goat cheese, crumbled

Directions

1. Preheat the oven to 400 degrees F.
2. Line a baking sheet with foil paper.
3. In a large bowl, add all ingredients except cheese and toss to coat well.
4. Place the sliced summer squash on baking sheet in a single layer.
5. Roast for about 15 to 16 minutes turning after about 8 minutes.
6. Transfer the roasted squash in a serving plate.
7. Spread the crumbled cheese over roasted squash and serve.

Serve this roasted summer squash with the sprinkling of some chopped fresh thyme.

Garlic Roasted Brussels Sprout

This is a very easy recipe which carries a very nice flavor and great nutrients. With cancer-protection and cholesterol-lowering benefits from the Brussels, this dish is a healthy choice every time.

Servings: 4
Prep Time: 10 minutes
Cooking Time: 40 minutes

1½ pounds Brussels sprout, trimmed
2 tablespoons coconut butter, melted
2 garlic cloves, crushed
1 teaspoon dried basil, crushed
Flaked sea salt and black pepper, to taste

Directions

1. Preheat the oven to 450 degrees F. Line a baking sheet with foil paper.
2. In a large bowl, add all ingredients and toss to coat well.
3. Place the Brussels sprout in prepared baking sheet.
4. Roast for about 35 to 40 minutes. Flip after every 6 to 7 minutes.
5. Serve this dish with fresh lemon slices.

Zucchini Stew Medley

This lovely zucchini dish is a good treat for the prostate, helps in the prevention of cancer and lowering of the cholesterol, blood sugar and blood sugar. On top of that, this dish may keep you feeling full for quite a while.

Serves: 4
Prep Time: 15 minutes
Cooking Time: 45 minutes

---

1 cup thinly sliced onions
2 pounds (906 grams) zucchini, scrubbed lightly and not pared then sliced paper thin
1 cup diced fresh tomatoes
¼ teaspoon freshly ground pepper
½ teaspoon oregano
4 tablespoons extra-virgin coconut oil
1 clove garlic, minced
1 green bell pepper, thinly sliced into julienne strips
1½ teaspoon flaked sea salt

Directions

1. Heat the oil in a skillet or frying pan.
2. Sauté onions and garlic on medium flame for about 5 minutes.
3. Add zucchini and green pepper. Sauté for 10 minutes while stirring regularly.
4. Mix in tomatoes, salt, ground pepper, oregano.
5. Cover and cook over low heat, 20 to 30 minutes while stirring at intervals.

Nutty Green Beans

This recipe has lime in it which gives a wonderfully light and lovely fresh touch, and walnuts which are a good source of healthy fats and adds a delicious crunch to green beans.

Servings: *4*
Prep Time: *10 minutes*
Cooking Time: *10 minutes*

---

1 pound (453 grams) fresh green beans, trimmed
¼ cup walnuts, toasted and chopped
1 tablespoon extra-virgin olive oil
1 teaspoon fresh lime juice
½ teaspoon lime zest, grated freshly
Flaked sea salt and black pepper, to taste

Directions

1. In a water filled pan, add beans and cook for 6 to 8 minutes or until tender.
2. Drain well. Place in a serving bowl.
3. Add remaining ingredients and mix well.
4. Serve warm.
5. Serve with fresh lime wedges.

Baked Spicy Carrots & Cauliflower

This dish is really simple and you can prepare it with just common ingredients that you may have in your pantry. The herbs and spices add a brilliant taste to the vegetables.

Serves: *4*
Prep Time: *10 minutes*
Cooking Time: *35 minutes*

---

1 large head of cauliflower, chopped roughly
1 onion, diced
1 carrot, peeled and diced
1 tablespoon extra-virgin olive oil
½ teaspoon dried oregano
½ teaspoon dried thyme
½ teaspoon dried marjoram
1 teaspoon red pepper flakes, crushed
1 teaspoon cayenne pepper
1 teaspoon smoked paprika
Flaked sea salt and black pepper, to taste

Directions

1. Preheat the oven to 375 degrees F.
2. In a large bowl, add all ingredients and toss to coat well.
3. Place the vegetables in a baking dish.
4. Bake for about 30 to 35 minutes.
5. Garnish these baked vegetables with chopped fresh rosemary.

Olive Grilled Asparagus

This asparagus recipe offers a fiber-rich meal that also contains anti-aging and anti-cancer properties. Healthy and tasty eating doesn't get easier than this.

Serves: 2
Prep Time: 10 minutes
Cooking Time: 10 minutes

½ pound (226 grams) asparagus, trimmed off tough parts and sliced
1 tablespoon extra-virgin olive oil
Onion salt, to taste
Cayenne pepper, to taste
Black pepper, to taste

Directions

1. Preheat the grill on medium heat
2. In a bowl, place the asparagus and remaining ingredients and toss to coat well.
3. Grill the asparagus for about 8 to 10 minutes.
4. Serve grilled asparagus with poached or boiled free-range eggs.

Baked Cheesy Summer Squash

*This wonderful summer squash cake is awesome in flavor and texture.
It is great even if guests are around and it is also a nice way to your
veggies.*

Servings: *4*
Prep Time: *10 minutes*
Cooking Time: *20 minutes*

---

*1 pound (453 grams) summer squash, seeded, grated and squeezed
finely
½ cup mozzarella cheese, grated freshly
1 tablespoon fresh basil, chopped
2/3 cup onion, chopped finely
1 large free-range egg, beaten
Flaked sea salt and black pepper, to taste
1 tablespoon extra-virgin coconut oil*

Directions

1. Preheat the oven to 400 degrees F. Lightly, grease a baking pan.
2. In a large bowl, add grated summer squash and cheese and mix.
3. In another bowl, add remaining ingredients except oil and mix well.
4. Mix cheese mixture into egg mixture.
5. In a non-stick pan, heat oil on medium heat.
6. Fill 1/3 of a cup with mixture and place in the pan.
7. Slightly, press down to make a 3-inch cake.
8. Cook for about 3 to 4 minutes or until golden brown.

9. Repeat with the remaining mixture.
10. Transfer the cakes into prepared pan.
11. Bake for about 10 minutes.
12. Serve this cake with avocado slices.

Stir-Fry Baby Bok Choy & Bell Pepper

The fresh vegetables in this recipe make a wonderfully delicious veggie stir-fry. This recipe is a good way to enjoy the delicate and crisp taste of bok choy.

Serves: *4*
Prep Time: *10 minutes*
Cooking Time: *10 minutes*

1½ tablespoons extra-virgin coconut oil
2 garlic cloves, minced
4 scallions, chopped
1 red bell pepper, seeded and diced
1 yellow bell pepper, seeded and diced
1 pound (453 grams) baby bok choy, trimmed and torn
Flaked sea salt to taste

Directions

1. In a large pan, heat oil on medium-high heat.
2. Add garlic and sauté for 30 seconds.
3. Add scallions and bell peppers and cook, stirring often for about 2 to 3 minutes.
4. Add bok choy and cook for 4 to 5 minutes or until wilted.
5. Serve with fresh lime wedges or your favorite cooked protein.

POULTRY

Creamy Tomato Chicken Stew

Enjoy this dish which is absolutely delicious and different from traditional chicken stew recipes. This delicious stew combines chicken, carrot and almond butter with a spicy touch from a medley of spices.

Serves: 2
Prep Time: 10 minutes
Cooking Time: 40 minutes

---

1 tablespoon organic ghee
1 small white onions, chopped
2 garlic cloves, chopped finely
2 free-range boneless chicken thighs, cubed
1½ cups gluten-free chicken broth
3 small carrots, peeled and cubed
1 cup home-made tomato puree
¼ teaspoon coriander powder
¼ teaspoon cumin powder
Chili powder, to taste
¼ cup almond butter
Flaked sea salt to taste

Directions

1. In a large pan, heat ghee on medium heat.
2. Add onion and sauté for about 4 to 5 minutes.
3. Add garlic and sauté for 1 minute more.
4. Add chicken and cook for 4 to 5 minutes.
5. Add remaining all ingredients except butter.
6. Bring to a boil and reduce the heat to medium-low.
7. Cover and simmer for about 15 to 20 minutes.
8. Uncover and simmer for about 10 minutes or until the liquid becomes thick.
9. In the last minute, add almond butter and stir until well mixed.
10. Garnish this stew with chopped fresh coriander.

Fruity Turkey Patties

This recipe makes it easy to make your own patty sausage with just a few healthy ingredients like ground turkey and natural seasonings. These patties are easy to make and great for lunch or maybe even breakfast.

Servings: *4*
Prep Time: *5 minutes*
Cooking Time: *20 minutes*

---

2 teaspoons extra-virgin coconut oil plus extra for cooking
1 onion, chopped
1 apple, peeled, cored and chopped
1 pound (453 grams) range free ground turkey
1 tablespoon fresh basil, chopped
1 tablespoon fresh sage, chopped
Pinch of smoked paprika
Flaked sea salt and black pepper, to taste

Directions

1. In a non-stick skillet, heat oil on medium heat.
2. Add onion and sauté for about 2 minutes.
3. Add apple and cook, stirring for 2 minutes further.
4. Transfer the apple mixture in a large bowl. Let it cool completely.
5. Add in remaining ingredients and mix until well combined.
6. Coat a clean non-stick frying pan with oil and heat on medium heat.

7. Shape the mixture into patties.
8. Add 2 patties in pan and cook for 3 to 4 minutes from both sides.
9. Repeat with other patties.
10. Serve these patties with fresh greens.

Yellow Chicken with Cauliflower Rice

This dish is loaded with nutrients to boost the immune system, prevent cancer, guard against Alzheimer's and more. Enjoy.

Serves: *4*
Prep Time: *10 minutes*
Cooking Time: *20 minutes*

For Yellow Chicken:
1 tablespoon organic ghee
1 small onion, sliced
2 cloves garlic, chopped
1 pound (453 grams) boneless chicken, cubed
½ cup cooked pumpkin, mashed
2/3 cup organic unsweetened coconut milk
1 teaspoon cumin powder
¼ teaspoon red pepper flakes, crushed
¼ teaspoon cayenne pepper
2 teaspoons turmeric powder
Flaked sea salt and black pepper, to taste
½ cup cashews

For Cauliflower Rice:
1 head cauliflower, removed stem and chopped roughly
1 tablespoon extra-virgin coconut oil
Pinch of flaked sea salt
¼ cup unsweetened coconut, shredded
1/3 cup organic coconut milk

Directions

1. To cook the yellow chicken: in a large skillet, heat

ghee on medium heat.

2. Add onion and sauté for 3 to 4 minutes.
3. Add garlic and sauté for 1 minute more.
4. Add chicken and cook, stirring for 3 to 4 minutes.
5. Add pumpkin and coconut milk and cook, stirring for 2 to 3 minutes or until pumpkin breaks down.
6. Add all spices and cook for 4 to 5 minutes or until sauce thicken.
7. Stir in cashews.
8. Meanwhile, in a food processor, add cauliflower and pulse until rice consistency forms.
9. In another pan, heat oil on medium-low heat.
10. Add cauliflower rice and salt. Cover and cook, stirring occasionally for 3 to 4 minutes.
11. Add shredded coconut and coconut milk and mix well.
12. Cover and cook, stirring occasionally for about 6 to 8 minutes or until all liquid is absorbed.
13. In a serving plate, place rice and then yellow chicken on top and serve.
14. Serve this dish with the garnishing of chopped fresh cilantro.

Creamy Chicken & Avocado Soup

Avocado gives a creamy texture to this chicken soup. This creamy soup also has a gorgeous color that makes it even more perfect.

Servings: 2
Prep Time: 10 minutes
Cooking Time: 20 minutes

1 tablespoon extra-virgin olive oil
3 fresh jalapeño peppers, seeded and sliced
6 garlic cloves, chopped finely
1 onion, chopped finely
½ pound (226 grams) boneless chicken, cubed
2 cups reduced-sodium and gluten-free chicken broth
1 tomato, seeded and chopped finely
1 tablespoon fresh lime juice
Flaked sea salt and black pepper, to taste
1 avocado, peeled, pitted and chopped

Directions

1. In a large soup pot, heat oil on medium heat.
2. Sauté jalapeño peppers, garlic and onion for about 4 to 5 minutes.
3. Add chicken and cook for 2 to 3 minutes.
4. Add broth, tomato and lime juice and bring to a boil.
5. Reduce the heat to medium-low and simmer for about 8 to 10 minutes.
6. Stir in avocado and heat completely.
7. Top this soup with chopped cilantro.

Easy Chicken Rosemary

This chicken dish is super easy to cook and also delivers a tangy taste from the lime juice.

Serves: 4
Prep Time: 10 minutes
Cooking Time: 15 minutes

---

4 boneless chicken breast halves
1 tablespoon extra-virgin olive oil
¼ cup fresh lime juice
2 tablespoons dried rosemary, crushed
Flaked sea salt and black pepper, to taste

Directions

1. In a bowl, add chicken, oil, lime juice and dried rosemary. Season with flaked sea salt and black pepper and toss to coat well.
2. Cover and refrigerate to marinate for about 6 to 8 hours. (optional, but works best)
3. Preheat the grill to medium-high heat then grease the grill grate lightly.
4. Discard the extra marinade from chicken.
5. Place the chicken halves on grill and cook for about 8 minutes from both sides.
6. Serve this grilled chicken with fresh lime wedges or some steamed green veggies.

Herbed Cheesy Chicken Wings

This dish is great dish for lunch or even on special occasions. Try this for one of the crispiest and healthiest chicken wings recipes.

Servings: *4*
Prep Time: *10 minutes*
Cooking Time: *45 minutes*

---

2 pounds (907 grams) free-range chicken wings
½ teaspoon dried thyme, crushed
½ teaspoon dried rosemary, crushed
½ teaspoon dried oregano, crushed
½ teaspoon cumin powder
Flaked sea salt and black pepper, to taste
2 tablespoons fresh basil, chopped finely
2 tablespoons extra-virgin olive oil
¼ cup Parmesan cheese

Directions

1. Preheat the oven to 425 degrees F.
2. Line a baking sheet with parchment paper.
3. In a bowl, add chicken wings, dried herbs, cumin, salt and black pepper and toss to coat well.
4. Place the chicken wings with coating in prepared baking dish.
5. Bake for about 35 to 45 minutes.
6. Meanwhile, in a bowl, add basil, oil, cheese and a pinch of salt and mix well.
7. Pour the cheese mixture over chicken and serve.
8. Serve these baked chicken wings with fresh greens.

Curried Turkey Meatballs

This tasty dish will receive a warm welcome in your home. Tender, moist and delicious turkey meatballs bring a great taste from the simple curry flavor.

Serves: *4*
Prep Time: *10 minutes*
Cooking Time: *15 minutes*

For Turkey Meatballs:
1 pound (453 grams) free-range ground turkey
2 free-range eggs, beaten
2/3 cup almond flour
1 small onion, chopped finely
½ teaspoon fresh ginger, minced
2 teaspoons curry powder
Pinch of cayenne pepper
Flaked sea salt and black pepper, to taste

For Curry Sauce:
2 tablespoons extra-virgin coconut oil
1 small onion, diced
1 clove garlic, minced
1 teaspoon fresh ginger, minced
2 cups organic coconut milk
1 cup gluten-free chicken broth
3 teaspoons curry powder
I teaspoon cumin powder
1 teaspoon coriander powder

Directions

1. In a large bowl, add all meatballs ingredients and mix until well combined.
2. Make balls from mixture according to desired size.
3. In a skillet, heat oil on medium heat.
4. Add onion and sauté for 3 to 4 minutes.
5. Add garlic and ginger and sauté for 1 minute more.
6. Add meatballs and cook for 3 to 4 minutes from all sides.
7. Add remaining curry sauce ingredients and mix well.
8. Bring to a boil and reduce the heat to medium-low.
9. Cover and simmer for about 5 minutes or until the sauce becomes thick.
10. Garnish this curry with chopped fresh basil.

Baked Chicken & Broccoli

This is a very satisfying dish and a good pick for a nice and quick last minute meal.

Serves: 4
Prep Time: 10 minutes
Cooking Time: 25 minutes

---

4 free-range chicken thighs
4 to 5 broccoli heads, cut into florets
1 tablespoon Italian seasoning
1 teaspoon garlic powder
Flaked sea salt and black pepper, to taste
2 tablespoons raw coconut vinegar
4 tablespoons extra-virgin coconut oil

Directions

1. Preheat the oven to 375 degrees F. Line a baking dish with parchment paper.
2. Place all ingredients in baking dish and toss to coat well.
3. Bake for 20 to 25 minutes.
4. Top this dish with grated cheese of your choice (no blue cheeses allowed).

Roasted Chicken Drumsticks with Fennel

Make this gorgeous and complete meal for a lavish dinner! This dish not only tastes great, but also fills the kitchen with a wonderful aroma.

Serves: *4*
Prep Time: *10 minutes*
Cooking Time: *30 minutes*

---

3 cups bulb fennel, cored and chopped
5 teaspoons extra-virgin coconut oil, divided
2 cloves garlic, minced
½ tablespoon fresh lime zest, freshly grated
2 tablespoons fresh sage leaves chopped
½ tablespoon fresh lime juice
Flaked sea salt and black pepper, to taste
1½ pounds (680 grams) free-range chicken drumsticks
2 tablespoons pine nuts

Directions

1. Preheat the oven to 450 degrees F.
2. In a baking dish, place fennel. Drizzle 2 teaspoons of oil and toss to coat well.
3. Bake for about 10 minutes.
4. Meanwhile in a blender add, garlic, lime zest, sage, lime juice, salt and black pepper and pulse until a smooth paste forms.
5. In a bowl, add paste, 1 teaspoon of oil and chicken drumsticks and coat well

6. In a non-stick skillet, heat remaining oil on medium-high heat.
7. Add chicken and cook, turning occasionally for about 4 to 5 minutes.
8. After the fennels are roasted for 10 minutes, mix in pine nuts.
9. Place the chicken over fennel.
10. Roast for 15 to 20 minutes further.
11. Serve this dish with fresh greens.

Chicken Kabobs

This is an easy and nutritious way to enjoy your chicken. Surely these extremely flavorful chicken kabobs will be a hit for any BBQ as well.

Servings: *4*
Prep Time: *1 hour 10 minutes*
Cooking Time: *15 minutes*

1½ pounds (680 grams) free-range boneless chicken, cubed
3 tablespoons extra-virgin olive oil
1 teaspoon fresh lemon juice
1 tablespoon raw coconut vinegar
½ teaspoon onion powder
½ teaspoon garlic powder
Flaked sea salt and black pepper, to taste
Red chili powder, to taste
1 teaspoon cumin powder

Amino Acd (soy sauce) ground ginger honey green onions

Directions

1. In a bowl, add chicken and all ingredients and stir to coat well.
2. Cover and refrigerate to marinate for about 1 hour.
3. Preheat the grill to medium-high heat.
4. Lightly grease the grill.
5. Thread the chicken in skewers. Discard the marinade.
6. Grill the skewers for 10 to 15 minutes.
7. Serve this chicken with fresh veggie salad.

Zucchini Lasagna with Chicken & Ricotta

This spring flavored zucchini and chicken lasagna makes a great meal. Quite an easy recipe to prepare and it tastes really delicious.

Servings: 4
Prep Time: 15 minutes
Cooking Time: 1 hour 25 minutes

For Sauce:
2 cups tomatoes
2 tablespoons extra-virgin olive oil
¼ teaspoon red pepper flakes
1 cup onion, chopped finely
2 garlic cloves, chopped finely
1 pound (453 grams) free-range ground chicken
Flaked sea salt, to taste
2 tablespoon fresh oregano, chopped finely

For Lasagna:
2 large zucchinis, trimmed and sliced into thin strips
¼ teaspoon extra-virgin olive oil
1 cup low-fat ricotta cheese, grated

Directions

For Sauce:
1. In a blender, add tomatoes and 1 cup of water and pulse until a paste forms.
2. In a non-stick skillet, heat oil on medium heat.

3. Add pepper flakes, onion and garlic and allow to sauté while also stirring often for approximately 6 to 8 minutes.
4. Add chicken and cook for about 4 o 5 minutes.
5. Add tomato paste and bring to a boil.
6. Reduce the heat to medium-low.
7. Simmer for about 15 to 20 minutes or until it thickens.
8. Add salt and oregano and stir well.
9. Keep aside to cool.

For Lasagna:
1. Preheat the oven to 375 degrees F.
2. Place 13 of slices zucchini in the bottom of baking dish.
3. Pour half of sauce over zucchini slices.
4. Sprinkle ¼ cup of cheese.
5. Repeat the layer, with zucchini, remaining sauce and ½ cup cheese. Place remaining zucchini on top.
6. Brush with olive oil.
7. Sprinkle remaining cheese on top.
8. Bake for 50 to 60 minutes.
9. While serving, garnish this lasagna with chopped fresh oregano.

Chicken Veggie Stew

This is a nice and hearty stew for a great dinner. The spice combination used contributes very well to the hearty flavor of this hearty stew.

Serves: *2*
Prep Time: *20 minutes*
Cooking Time: *30 minutes*

¼ cup almonds
2 tablespoons water
1 tablespoon of extra-virgin coconut oil
1 small onion, diced
1 garlic clove, chopped
2 boneless free-range chicken breasts, cut into bite size pieces
½ pound (226 grams) mushrooms, diced
½ parsnip, peeled and cubed
2 stalks celery, diced
2 cups water
1 bay leaf
½ teaspoon dried rosemary
½ teaspoon dried thyme
¼ teaspoon cayenne pepper
Flaked sea salt and black pepper, to taste

Directions

1. In a bowl, soak almonds in water for 10 minutes and then puree them. Keep aside.
2. In a large pan, add oil and heat on medium heat.
3. Add onion and sauté for 3 to 4 minutes.
4. Add garlic and sauté for 1 minute more.

5. Add remaining ingredients except almond puree. Cover and cook for about 10 to 15 minutes.
6. Add almond puree and cook for10 minutes more or until stew thickens.
7. Garnish the stew with chopped fresh parsley.

Orange Herbed Chicken Thighs

The chicken thighs in this recipe boast a fresh orange taste. This herbed chicken thigh recipe offers a flavorful chicken dinner.

Serves: 4
Prep Time: 10 minutes plus overnight refrigeration
Cooking Time: 10 minutes

---

2 cups freshly squeezed orange juice
2 garlic cloves, chopped
¼ cup fresh cilantro, chopped
1 small onion, chopped
1 teaspoon dried thyme
1 teaspoon dried rosemary
1 teaspoon dried marjoram
½ teaspoon chili pepper
Flaked sea salt and black pepper, to taste
2 pounds (907 grams) free-range boneless chicken thighs
1 tablespoon extra-virgin coconut oil

Directions

1. In a blender, add all ingredients except oil and chicken and blend until a smooth paste forms.
2. In a bowl, add chicken and marinade and mix well.
3. Cover and refrigerate to marinate overnight.
4. In a large non-stick skillet, heat oil on medium-high heat.
5. Discard extra marinade and place chicken in the skillet.
6. Cook chicken thighs for 5 minutes per side.

7. Serve this chicken with fresh green salad.

FISH & SEAFOOD

Spicy Coconut Shrimp Soup

This hearty soup is filled with lots of spicy flavors. The creamy coconut milk gives this soup extra tasty flavor and overall this soup is uplifting.

Serves: 4
Prep Time: 10 minutes
Cooking Time: 18 minutes

---

2 tablespoons extra-virgin coconut oil
¾ cup white onion, chopped
2 garlic cloves, chopped
2 jalapeño peppers, diced
1½ cups tomatoes, chopped finely
¼ cup fresh cilantro, chopped
2 pounds (907 grams) wild shrimps, cleaned and deveined
1½ cups organic coconut milk
1 tablespoon fresh lemon juice
Flaked sea salt and black pepper, to taste

Directions

1. In a pan, heat oil on medium heat.
2. Add onion and sauté for 2 to 3 minutes.
3. Add garlic and jalapeño and sauté for 1 to 2 minute s more.
4. Add tomato and cilantro and cook, stirring for 2 to 3 minutes.
5. Add shrimps and reduce the heat to medium-low.
6. Simmer for 4 to 5 minutes.
7. Add coconut milk and simmer for 4 to 5 minutes more.
8. In the last minute, add lemon juice.
9. Season with salt and black pepper.
10. Serve this soup with avocado slices.

Wild Salmon with Arugula Pesto Salad

This is a fresh and light meal for lunch. All flavors of this healthy wild salmon and arugula pesto are nicely combined to make this nice dish.

Serves: 4
Prep Time: 20 minutes
Cooking Time: 5 minutes

For Arugula Pesto:
2 cups fresh arugula
¼ cup pecans
2 small garlic cloves
½ cup extra-virgin olive oil
Flaked sea salt and black pepper, to taste

For Salad:
½ cup white cabbage shredded
½ cup red cabbage, shredded
3 cups baby spinach
1 cup green beans, cooked and chopped
1 cup rocket leaves
1 cup lettuce leaves
¼ cup edible pumpkin seeds

For Salmon:
4 wild salmon fillets
1 teaspoon dried thyme
1 teaspoon dried oregano
Flaked sea salt and black pepper, to taste

Directions

1. In a food processor, add all pesto ingredients except oil and pulse until chopped finely.
2. Gradually, add oil and pulse until smooth.
3. Cover and refrigerate.
4. In a large bowl, add all ingredients of salad and mix well.
5. Refrigerate until fish is prepared.
6. Preheat the broiler. Line a baking sheet with foil paper.
7. Place fish on baking sheet. Sprinkle thyme, oregano, salt and black pepper and coat well.
8. Place 1 tablespoon of pesto over fish fillets evenly.
9. Cook fillets under broiler for about 5 minutes or until opaque.
10. Serve this fish with prepared salad.

Tangy Garlic Grilled Fish

This is a quick and easy grilled fish dish which is also nutritious. This refreshing and light grilled fish has the delicate flavors of vinegar, lemon and garlic.

Serves: 2
***Prep Time:** 10 minutes plus refrigeration time*
***Cooking Time:** 10 minutes*

---

2 wild fish fillets (such as herring, salmon and haddock etc.)
Fresh juice of 1 lemon
1 tablespoon raw coconut vinegar
1 tablespoon extra-virgin coconut oil
2 small cloves garlic, crushed
Flaked sea salt and black pepper, to taste
Pinch of cayenne pepper

Directions

1. In a bowl, add fish and all ingredients and toss to coat well.
2. Cover and refrigerate to marinate for about 1 to 2 hours.
3. Preheat the grill for medium. Lightly, grease the grill grate.
4. Place the fish on grill and cook for 4 to 5 minutes per side.
5. Serve this fish with avocado salsa, lettuce leaves or fresh greens.

Marinated Grilled Salmon with Lemon Sauce

This simple but flavorful marinade gives the salmon fish a super tasty touch. This recipe is a perfect dish to try even if you don't like fish.

Servings: *4*
Prep Time: *1 hour 5 minutes*
Cooking Time: *10 minutes*

¼ cup balsamic vinegar
1 tablespoon fresh rosemary, chopped finely and divided
4 garlic cloves, minced
Cayenne pepper, to taste
Flaked sea salt and black pepper, to taste
4 (4-ounce each) wild salmon fillets
1 tablespoon extra-virgin olive oil
1 tablespoon fresh lemon juice

Directions

1. In a bowl, add vinegar, half of rosemary, garlic, cayenne pepper, salt and black pepper and mix well.
2. Add fish fillets and toss to coat well.
3. Cover and refrigerate to marinate for about 1 hour.
4. Meanwhile, in a bowl, add oil, lemon juice and remaining rosemary and mix well.
5. Preheat the grill. Lightly, grease the griddle.
6. Place the fish on griddle and cook for about 10 minutes turning once.
7. Place the fish on serving platter. Pour lemon sauce over fish and serve.

Black Cod with Artichokes & Lemon

This is such an easy throw-together meal for dinner. Before you know it, this dish could become one of your favorite.

Serves: *4*
Prep Time: *10 minutes*
Cooking Time: *15 minutes*

---

2 tablespoons extra-virgin coconut oil, divided
1 small onion, sliced thinly
2 garlic cloves, chopped
4 baby artichoke hearts halved
2 tablespoons fresh basil, chopped
1 lemon, sliced thinly
1½ pounds (680 grams) wild black cod fillets, cubed
Flaked sea salt and black pepper, to taste

Directions

1. In a large non-stick pan, heat 1 tablespoon of oil on medium heat.
2. Add onion and garlic and sauté for 2 to 3 minutes.
3. Add artichokes, basil and lemon slices.
4. Reduce the heat to medium-low. Cover and cook for 6 to 7 minutes.
5. Transfer the artichoke mixture to a plate.
6. In the same skillet heat remaining oil.
7. Add fish, salt and black peppers and cook, stirring occasionally for about 4 to 5 minutes.
8. Add artichoke mixture in skillet, mix well and heat completely.

Crusty Baked Fish

This baked fish is a great way to get those healthy proteins into your diet. The double coating of the eggs and the coconut mixture in this dish provides a thick and tasty crust for the trout fillet.

Serves: 4
Prep Time: 10 minutes
Cooking Time: 25-30 minutes

---

1 pound (453 grams) wild trout fillet
1 large free-range eggs
3 tablespoons gluten-free fish stock or water
1 cup coconut flour
Flaked sea salt and pepper to taste
Seasonings of your choice according to taste - tarragon, basil, oregano, thyme etc.

Directions

1. Preheat your oven to 350 degrees Fahrenheit and prepare a baking dish with grass fed butter or extra-virgin coconut oil.
2. In a dish, combine the egg and fish stock or water.
3. On a piece of waxed paper or in a dish, combine the coconut flour, sea salt, pepper and other seasonings of your choice.
4. Dip each trout fillet into the egg mixture and then coat it in the coconut flour mix. Create a double coating by repeating these steps.
5. Place the coated fish into the prepared baking dish.

6. Bake the fish until it becomes golden brown for about 10-15 minutes on each side.
7. Serve warm with your favorite steamed veggies or avocado slices.

Zesty Garlic Shrimp

This is tasty shrimp recipe results in an interesting mix of flavors from the garlic, coconut oil, cilantro and lime juice. Treat your taste buds with this flavorful shrimp dish.

Serves: 2
Prep Time: 10 minutes
Cooking Time: 15 minutes

---

1 pound (453 grams) shrimp, peeled and deveined
2 tablespoons extra-virgin coconut oil
2 chili peppers, thinly sliced into rings
3 cloves garlic, sliced thinly
Flaked sea salt to taste
¼ cup cilantro, chopped
2 tablespoons freshly squeezed lime juice

Directions

1. Place a skillet on medium-high heat. After the skillet heats up for about a minute, add the olive oil. Heat the oil until it becomes almost smoky.
2. Add the chili to the heated oil and stir well for ½ minute. Stir in the shrimp and thinly sliced garlic then add a dash of sea salt. Toss to combine well. Cook for about a minute before tossing again. Frequently stir the shrimp for about 3-4 minutes until it is cooked.
3. Remove the heat and add in the chopped cilantro, then the tablespoons of freshly squeezed lime juice.
4. Serve with your favorite non-starchy veggies.

Grilled Shrimps with Herbs

This is an awesome recipe for a tasty grilled shrimp lunch or even dinner. The herbs, along with the remaining marinade add a nice burst of flavor to shrimps.

Serves: 4
Prep Time: 10 minutes
Cooking Time: 10 minutes

---

2 pounds (907 grams) shrimps, peeled and deveined
½ cup extra-virgin coconut oil
¼ cup fresh basil, chopped
3 cloves garlic
1 teaspoon dried thyme
1 teaspoon dried oregano
Flaked sea salt and black pepper
1 tablespoon of home-made tomato puree

Directions

1. In a bowl, add all ingredients and toss to coat well.
2. Cover and refrigerate to marinate for 2 hours.
3. Preheat the grill to medium-low heat.
4. Grease the grill, lightly.
5. Thread the shrimps on skewers. Discard the extra marinade.
6. Place on the grill and cook for 4 to 5 minutes from both sides.

Spicy Salmon Stew

This delicious salmon stew dish turns out to be hot and spicy based on the choice of chili and other spices. It makes a great meal to awake the taste buds.

Serves: 4
Prep Time: 10 minutes
Cooking Time: 35-45 minutes

---

2 pounds (453 grams) wild salmon fillets, boneless, skinless
1 tablespoon extra-virgin olive oil
4 ribs celery with leaves, sliced (divided)
5 garlic cloves, peel and whole
2 fresh red chili peppers, cut in half, ribs and seeds removed
1 bunch cilantro, stems removed and chopped in pieces
2 tablespoons paprika
1 teaspoon flaked sea salt
½ cup water

Directions

1. Grease the bottom of deep skillet pan with some of the extra-virgin olive oil. Add half of the celery ribs, all the garlic cloves and chili pepper.
2. Place the salmon fillet pieces on top of this vegetable layer. Add the remaining celery, cilantro, paprika and sea salt on top. Evenly pour the remaining olive oil on top of the seasonings. Pour in the water.
3. Cover the skillet while also leaving a vent for releasing some steam. Cook until the liquid reached boiling point. Lower the heat and allow simmering

for 15 to 18 minutes.

4. Garnish with cilantro and serve with your favorite salad.

Cherry Roasted Wild Herring

This a fish dish that is full of aromatic flavors. The finished dish will look great with the colors of the tomatoes and onion.

Servings: *4*
Prep Time: *10 minutes*
Cooking Time: *30 minutes*

---

2 tablespoons extra-virgin olive oil
2 large red onions, sliced into thin wedges
2 cups cherry tomatoes
Flaked sea salt and black pepper, to taste
4 wild herring fish fillets
1 tablespoon dried rosemary, crushed

Directions

1. Preheat the oven to 400 degrees F. Line 2 roasting dishes with foil paper.
2. In a prepared pan, place 1 tablespoon of oil, onions and tomatoes. Sprinkle with a little salt and black pepper and toss to coat well.
3. Roast for about 20 minutes.
4. Place the fish in other prepared pan. Coat with remaining oil, salt, pepper and rosemary.
5. Roast fish along with vegetables for about 8 to 10 minutes.
6. Serve the roasted fish, onion and tomatoes with the topping of home-made basil pesto.

Fish & Tomato Stew

This fish stew is quite delicious and easy to get going. This is essentially just a simple tomato based stew with fish in it.

Serves: 2
Prep Time: 10 minutes
Cooking Time: 20 minutes

---

3 tablespoons extra-virgin coconut oil
½ cup white onion, chopped
1 garlic clove, chopped
1 teaspoon home-made tomato paste
½ cup tomato, chopped finely
1/3 pound (150 grams) mixed wild fish fillets (cod, salmon, halibut and herring), cubed
2 tablespoons apple cider vinegar
6-ounce gluten-free fish broth
1 teaspoon mixed dried herbs (thyme, oregano and sage), crushed
Flaked sea salt and black pepper

Directions

1. In a pan, heat oil on medium-high heat.
2. Add onion and garlic and sauté for 2 to 3 minutes.
3. Add tomato paste and chopped tomato and cook, stirring occasionally for 6 to 7 minutes.
4. Add fish fillets, vinegar and broth and bring to a boil.
5. Reduce the heat to medium-low.
6. Simmer for about 6 to 7 minutes.
7. Sprinkle seasoning and herbs.
8. Serve this fish stew with the garnishing of chopped

fresh parsley.

Spicy Yellow Shrimps

This classic recipe is full of wonderful flavors. These are simple ingredients with a big taste.

Servings: 2
Prep Time: 10 minutes
Cooking Time: 15 minutes

---

2 tablespoons extra-virgin coconut oil
1 small onion, chopped very finely
2 small garlic cloves, minced
1 tomato, chopped very finely
Flaked sea salt and black pepper, to taste
¼ teaspoon turmeric powder
Paprika powder, to taste
1 teaspoon ground coriander
1 teaspoon ground cumin
1 cup water
½ pound (226 grams) jumbo shrimps, cleaned and deveined

Directions

1. In a skillet, heat oil on medium heat.
2. Add onion and sauté for 3 to 4 minutes.
3. Add garlic and sauté for 1 minute more.
4. Add tomato, salt, black pepper and remaining spices, and cook stirring continuously for about 4 to 5 minutes.
5. Add water and bring to a boil.
6. Reduce the heat to medium-low and stir in shrimps.
7. Cook for about 4 to 5 minutes or until shrimps are

done completely.

8. Serve this dish with the garnishing of chopped fresh cilantro.

BEEF, PORK, LAMB

Garlicky Beef Steak

This recipe is a healthy addition to your lunch. The flavors of butter and garlic make this steak mouthwatering and absolutely irresistible.

Serves: *4*
Prep Time: *10 minutes*
Cooking Time: *20 minutes*

---

2 pounds (907 grams) grass-fed round beef steak, cut into 1 ½-inch thick pieces
1 tablespoon almond butter or pasture-fed butter, melted
6 garlic cloves, crushed
Garlic salt, to taste
Black pepper, to taste

Directions

1. Preheat the grill for high. Lightly, grease the grill grate.

2. In a bowl, add beef and remaining things.
3. Rub the garlic mixture over beef evenly.
4. Place the beef steak on grill.
5. Cook for 10 minutes per side.
6. Serve this steak with fresh lime slices.

Curried Lamb Shanks & Apples

This delicious dish is great for a hearty and brainy family meal. The combination of lime, apple and spices gives these lamb shanks a nice rich flavor.

Serves: 2
Prep Time: *10 minutes*
Cooking Time: *2 hours 10 minutes*

---

2 tablespoons organic ghee
2 grass-fed lamb shanks
1½ cups onion, chopped
3 garlic cloves, crushed
½ teaspoon dried rhyme
½ teaspoon dried oregano
½ tablespoon cumin powder
½ tablespoon coriander powder
Flaked sea salt and black pepper, to taste
2 lime slices
1 cup gluten-free vegetable broth
1 cup apple, peeled, cored and chopped
5 small turnips, peeled and halved (optional)

Directions

1. Preheat the oven to 300 degrees F.
2. In an oven-proof pan, heat ghee on medium-high heat.
3. Add lamb shanks and cook for 4 to 5 minutes or until browned.
4. Remove lamb from pan.

5. In the same pan, add onion and garlic and sauté for 5 minutes.
6. Now, stir in lamb shanks, herbs, seasoning, lime slices, broth and apple.
7. Cover and place the pan in oven.
8. Bake for about 1 hour 30 minutes.
9. If using, stir in turnips and bake for additional 15-30 minutes more or until the meal is cooked.
10. Garnish this curry with chopped fresh rosemary.

Cheesy Beef Balls with Olives

This is a great dish of ground beef with cheese and seasoning that creates a bursting combination of flavors.

Servings: *4*
Prep Time: *15 minutes*
Cooking Time: *10 minutes*

---

1 pound (453 grams) grass-fed ground beef
½ cup goat cheese, crumbled
½ green olives, chopped
2 tablespoons red onion, chopped finely
½ cup fresh cilantro, chopped finely
2 free-range eggs, beaten
Smoked paprika, to taste
Flaked sea salt and black pepper, to taste

Directions

1. Preheat the broiler of oven.
2. Line a baking sheet with parchment paper.
3. In a large bowl, add all ingredients and mix well.
4. Make small balls from meat mixture.
5. Place the balls in lined baking sheet.
6. Broil for 3 to 4 minutes about 3-inches away from heat.
7. Flip the side of ball and broil for 3 to 4 minutes more.
8. Serve these balls with gluten-free home-made dip or with steamed veggies.

Gingery Turnip Beef Soup

With smooth almond butter and turnip, this adds a decadent and creamy texture to this beef soup. This soup is healthy for the whole family.

Servings: *4*
Prep Time: *10 minutes*
Cooking Time: *45 minutes*

---

1 teaspoon extra-virgin olive oil
1 small onion, chopped
2 garlic cloves, chopped finely
8-ounces (226 grams) grass-fed boneless beef, cut into thin strips
5 cups reduced sodium and gluten-free vegetable broth
2 cups turnip, peeled and diced
½ cup smooth almond butter
2 tablespoons fresh ginger, minced
¼ cup fresh basil, chopped
Flakes sea salt and black pepper, to taste

Directions

1. In a large soup pot, heat oil on medium heat.
2. Add onion and garlic and sauté for 2 to 3 minutes.
3. Add beef and cook for 4 to 5 minutes.
4. Add broth and turnips and bring to a boil.
5. Reduce the heat to medium-low. Cover and simmer for about 25 to 30 minutes.
6. In a bowl, add ½ cup of soup and butter and beat until smooth paste forms.
7. Add ginger and basil to the soup pot and bring to a

boil.

8. Reduce the heat and cover and simmer for about 5 minutes.
9. Add butter paste and stir well.
10. Season with salt and black pepper.
11. Serve with the squeezing of some fresh lime juice.

Lamb Chops with Roasted Cherry Tomatoes

This dish is very tasty and makes an easy main meal. Enjoy the mixture of roasted red onions and cherry tomatoes with these lamb chops.

Serves: *4*
Prep Time: *10 minutes*
Cooking Time: *25 minutes*

---

1 red onion, sliced
2 cups (or about 2 pounds/907 grams)) cherry tomatoes
2 tablespoons extra-virgin olive oil, divided
4 grass-fed lamb chops
½ tablespoon dried thyme, crushed
½ tablespoon dried oregano, crushed
Flaked sea salt and black pepper, to taste

Directions

1. Preheat the oven to 400 degrees Fahrenheit, Line a baking sheet with parchment paper.
2. In a pan, melt 1 tablespoon of coconut oil.
3. Place cherry tomatoes and onion on prepared baking sheet.
4. Pour melted oil over vegetables and coat well.
5. Bake for 15 to 20 minutes.
6. Meanwhile, in a non-stick skillet, heat remaining oil on medium-low heat.
7. Add chops and cook for 4 to 5 minutes.
8. Add thyme, oregano, salt and pepper and cook for 4

to 5 minutes more or until chops are done completely.

9. Serve chops with roasted tomatoes and onion.
10. Serve with topping of fresh rosemary.

Slow Cooker Pork Roast

This organic pork roast dish is great for the whole family. Indulge in a healthy protein dish that is bursting with flavors and good nutrition.

Serves 4-6
Prep Time: *10 minutes*
Cooking Time: *8-10 hours on low*

---

4 pounds (1.8 kg) boneless organic pork roast
1 cup bell peppers, finely chopped
1 teaspoon freshly grated lemon zest or rind
Flaked sea salt and pepper, to taste
6 cloves garlic, finely chopped
Dash of ground nutmeg
A sprig of thyme or 2 teaspoon dried thyme leaves
¼ cup of gluten-free vegetable stock

Directions

1. Season the pork roast with sea salt and pepper according to your liking, then transfer it to a 4½ quart slow cooker.
2. In a bowl, mix all of the remaining ingredients and evenly pour it over the pork roast.
3. Cover and cook on low for 8-10 hours or until it is cooked according to your slow cooker manual.
4. Serve with avocado or tomato slices or your favorite salad.

Go-Easy Steak

This steak fillet recipe is quick and truly easy which makes it perfect for a beginner. In addition, it is a healthy protein dish that makes a great dinner.

Serves: *2*
Prep Time: *5 minutes*
Cooking Time: *10 minutes*

---

2 large grass-fed steak fillets
3 tablespoons of extra-virgin coconut oil
Flakes sea salt and pepper to taste
Your favorite natural powdered herbs/spices (optional)

Directions

1. In a skillet, heat the coconut oil over medium flame.
2. Season the steak with sea salt, pepper and your choice of powdered herbs and spices if using. Place the seasoned steak fillet into the skillet and cook for about 3-5 minutes on each side. Remove the cooked steak from the pan.
3. Serve the steak with your favorite veggies/salad.

Spiced Ground Beef & Zucchini

*This stir fry dish combines beef and zucchini to make good nutrition.
Enjoy the spicy flavor in each bite.*

Serves: 2
Prep Time: 10 minutes
Cooking Time: 15 minutes

½ tablespoon organic ghee
1 small onion, chopped finely
2 garlic cloves, minced
¼ teaspoon fresh ginger, minced
½ pound (226 grams) grass-fed lean ground beef
1 small tomato, chopped finely
1 medium zucchini, diced
2 tablespoons fresh parsley
Flaked sea salt and black pepper, to taste
½ teaspoon turmeric powder
½ teaspoon coriander powder
½ teaspoon cumin powder
½ teaspoon smoked paprika

Directions

1. In a non-stick skillet, heat ghee on medium heat.
2. Add onion and sauté for 3 to 4 minutes.
3. Add garlic and ginger and sauté for 1 minute more.
4. Add ground beef and cook for 6 to 8 minutes.
5. Stir in tomato, zucchini, parsley and all spices.
6. Reduce the heat to medium-low.
7. Cover and cook for about 2 minutes or until zucchini

become tender.
8. Garnish with fresh chopped mint leaves.

Nutty Pork Chops

Healthy protein and healthy fats is the high point of this pork dish. With a slight sugary sauce, the nuts add a crunchy twist to this recipe.

Serves: *2*
Prep Time: *10 minutes*
Cooking Time: *25-30 minutes*

---

4 (about ¾-inch thickness) organic pork chops
3 tablespoons extra-virgin coconut oil, divided
1 tablespoon natural stevia
1/8 teaspoon ground cinnamon
1/8 teaspoon ground nutmeg
Flaked sea salt and pepper to taste
4 tablespoons walnuts or pecans

Directions

1. Place oven-safe casserole dish in a preheated warm oven of 175 degrees Fahrenheit.
2. Lightly brush pork chops with a tablespoon of coconut oil and place it in a hot skillet over medium-high heat. Cook for about 5 minutes on each side turning at intervals until cooked. Place cooked pork chops in the casserole dish in the preheated oven to keep it warm.
3. In the meantime, in a small bowl, mix together the following: natural stevia, pepper, sea salt, ground cinnamon and ground nutmeg. In the same skillet add the remaining coconut oil and stir in seasoned cinnamon mixture. Simmer covered for about 3-4

minutes on medium heat, then continue to cook uncovered until the sauce in skillet begins to slightly thicken. Pour sauce on pork chops and evenly layer with walnuts or pecans.

4. Serve immediately.

Grilled Spicy Beef Sausages

These sausages are spicy and also wonderful in flavors and texture. Have fun making these sausages and enjoy the healthy protein benefits.

***Serves:** 4*
***Prep Time:** 10 minutes*
***Cooking Time:** 10 minutes*

---

1 pound (453 grams) grass-fed ground beef
1 small white onion, chopped finely
½ tablespoon fresh ginger, minced very finely
¼ cup fresh cilantro, chopped
1 teaspoon green chili paste
1 teaspoon smoked paprika
Cayenne pepper, to taste
1 teaspoon coriander powder
1 teaspoon cumin powder
Flaked sea salt and black pepper, to taste
2 tablespoon extra-virgin olive oil

Directions

1. In a large bowl, add all ingredients except oil and mix until well combined.
2. Cover and refrigerate to marinate for about 2 to 3 hours.
3. Preheat the grill to high. Liberally, grease grill grate.
4. Thread sausages onto skewers.
5. Place skewers on grill and cook for about 10 minutes or until completely cooked.

Garlic Lamb & Chard

This recipe can be a regular weekday meal or whenever you wish. Enjoy.

Serves: *4*
Prep Time: *10 minutes*
Cooking Time: *15 minutes*

---

1 tablespoon extra-virgin coconut oil
1½ pounds lean lamb, diced
1 small onion, sliced thinly
2 cloves garlic, chopped
1 pack chard, trimmed
1 teaspoon cumin powder
1 teaspoon coriander powder
½ teaspoon turmeric powder
1½ cups gluten-free lamb or chicken stock

Directions

1. In a skillet, heat oil on medium-high heat.
2. Add lamb and stir fry for 5 to 6 minutes.
3. Add onion, garlic, chard and all spices and cook for 4 to 5 minutes.
4. Add broth and cook for 6 to 7 minutes.
5. Season with salt and black pepper.
6. Top with toasted pine nuts while serving (optional).

DESSERTS

Chocolate Pudding

This creamy pudding is a class among gluten-free desserts and has a rich coconut and chocolate flavor. This yummy chocolaty treat is surely a kid's favorite and will please adults as well. Plus, no cooking is required.

Serves: *4*
Prep Time: *5 minutes plus additional time for refrigeration*

---

1 cup coconut milk
½ tablespoon shredded coconut
1/3 cup chia seeds
2 tablespoons gluten-free cocoa powder

Directions

1. In a bowl, add all ingredients and mix well.
2. Cover and refrigerate for about 7 to 8 hours.
3. Remove from refrigerator and blend until creamy

and smooth.

4. Refrigerate to chill before serving.
5. Serve this pudding with dollop of coconut cream if you wish.

Blueberry Apple Cobbler

This is one of the tastier and healthier versions of traditional cobblers. This recipe has blueberries and apple perfectly nestled to create a very tasty cobbler.

Serves: 4
Prep Time: 10 minutes
Cooking Time: 1 hour

½ cup almond flour
1/3 teaspoon non-aluminum, gluten free baking powder
½ teaspoon flaked sea salt
3 tablespoons almond butter, melted
½ cup unsweetened almond milk
1 tablespoon natural stevia
½ teaspoon gluten-free vanilla extract
1 cup fresh blueberries
1½ cups apple, peeled, cored and sliced

Directions

1. Preheat the oven to 350 degrees F. Lightly, grease a baking dish.
2. In a bowl, add flour, baking powder and salt and mix well
3. In another bowl, add butter, milk, stevia and vanilla and beat until well combined.
4. Mix milk mixture into flour mixture.
5. Place the mixture in prepared pan.
6. Spread the apple and blueberries over flour mixture

evenly.

7. Bake for 50 to 60 minutes or until the top becomes golden brown.

8. Serve this cobbler with the dusting of cinnamon powder.

Vanilla Mixed Berries Ice Cream

This recipe easily satisfies that craving for regular ice cream in a healthy way. With this dessert, you'll be able to please kids, family and friends.

Serves: 4
Prep Time: *5 minutes plus additional time in the freezer*

---

2 cups frozen mixed berries* (raspberries, blackberries, strawberries, blueberries and cherries)
½ cup unsweetened almond milk
1 teaspoon organic vanilla extract
*Remember that flash frozen berries are always best

Directions

1. In a food processor, add berries and pulse until chopped finely.
2. Add remaining ingredients and pulse until soft ice cream consistency forms.
3. Transfer in a bowl.
4. Serve immediately or cover and freeze for 2 to 3 hours to chill completely.
5. Serve this ice cream with the chocolate shaving (having 70% or more cocoa).

Chocolate Cupcakes

This is a delicious recipe of chocolate cupcakes. These decadent cupcakes make an irresistible dessert or snack for chocolate lovers.

Serves: *4*
Prep Time: *10 minutes*
Cooking Time: *18 minutes*

¼ cup almond flour
¼ teaspoon non-aluminum baking soda
¼ cup gluten-free raw cacao powder
Dash of non-aluminum, gluten free baking powder
¼ teaspoon flaked sea salt
4 large free-range eggs
2 tablespoons natural stevia
¼ cup coconut oil, melted
2 teaspoons dark chocolate chips (70% or more cocoa)

Directions

1. Preheat the oven to 350 degrees F. Line a muffin cup tray with paper liner.
2. In a bowl, add flour, baking soda, baking powder, cocoa and salt and mix well.
3. In another bowl, add eggs, stevia and oil and beat until well combined.
4. Mix egg mixture into flour mixture.
5. Fold in chocolate chips.
6. Place the mixture in prepared muffins tray.
7. Bake for about 15 to 18 minutes or a toothpick inserted in the center comes out clean.

8. You may serve these cupcakes with the topping of pitted organic cherries.

Peachy Delight Sorbet

This is a perfect peachy treat to end a lavish lunch or dinner or satisfy that sweet tooth. Your family and friends will likely say yes to this treat.

Serves: *4*
Prep Time: *10 minutes*
Cooking Time: *3 minutes plus additional freezing time*

---

2 tablespoons fresh lemon juice
1 tablespoon natural stevia (optional)
1/3 cup water
4 large peaches, peeled, pitted and sliced

Directions

1. In a pan, add lemon juice, stevia and water.
2. Cook on medium heat for about 2 to 3 minutes.
3. Let it cool slightly.
4. Transfer the water mixture into a blender.
5. Add peach slices in blender and blend until smooth.
6. Place the mixture in an ice cream machine.
7. Freeze according to manufacturer's directions.
8. Now, transfer the sorbet into a container.
9. Cover and freeze until firm.
10. Serve with the topping of fresh mint leaves.

Lemon Cake

This cake is light and airy with fine texture. It also has a wonderful citrus flavor that comes from adding the lemon zest.

Serves: *4*
Prep Time: *10 minutes*
Cooking Time: *35 minutes*

1½ cups almond flour
2 teaspoons non-aluminum, gluten free baking powder (optional –
omitting this will affect airy texture)
Pinch of cinnamon powder
¼ teaspoon cardamom powder
2 tablespoons lemon zest, grated freshly
2 teaspoons natural stevia, divided
4 free-range eggs, separated yolks and whites
1 teaspoon apple cider vinegar
Pinch of flaked sea salt

Directions

1. Preheat the oven to 350 degrees F. Line a cake pan with parchment paper and grease.
2. In a large bowl, add flour, baking powder, cinnamon and cardamom and mix well.
3. In another bowl-, add lemon zest, 1 teaspoon stevia and egg yolks and beat well.
4. Mix egg yolk mixture into flour mixture.
5. In a third bowl, add egg whites and beat well.
6. Gradually, add vinegar and salt and beat until soft peaks form.

7. Gently, fold the egg whites mixture in flour mixture.
8. Place the cake mixture in prepared pan.
9. Bake for 35 minutes or until a toothpick inserted in the center comes out clean.
10. Serve this cake with chopped almonds.

Pumpkin Custard

This pumpkin custard is an easy-to-make dessert with ingredients that may be easily available in your kitchen. This unique dessert will be a great hit with the whole family.

***Serves:** 2*
***Prep Time:** 10 minutes*
***Cooking Time:** 5 minutes*

½ cup almond milk
½ cup pumpkin, cooked and pureed
Natural stevia, to taste
¼ teaspoon gluten-free vanilla extract
¼ teaspoon cinnamon powder
Pinch of gluten-free allspice powder
1 tablespoon warm water
¼ tablespoon gluten-free gelatin powder

Directions

1. In a pan, add almond milk, pureed pumpkin, stevia, vanilla, cinnamon and all spice and cook, stirring for about 4 to 5 minutes or until smooth. Remove from heat.
2. In a bowl, mix together warm water and gelatin powder.
3. Stir gelatin into pumpkin mixture and beat until well combined.
4. Chill for about 3 to 4 hours before serving.
5. Serve this custard with the topping of chopped almonds.

Coconut Lemon Macaroons

Coconut adds a rich nutty flavor plus good fat in these macaroons. This recipe is also popular with kids.

Serves: *2*
Prep Time: *10 minutes*
Cooking Time: *12 minutes*

½ tablespoon flaxseed powder
½ tablespoon coconut flour
1 cup coconut flakes, shredded finely
2 tablespoons natural stevia
2 tablespoons extra-virgin coconut oil
¼ teaspoon gluten-free vanilla extract
½ teaspoon fresh lemon juice
½ lemon zest, grated freshly
2 tablespoons almonds, toasted and chopped very finely
½ tablespoon water
¼ teaspoon flaked sea salt

Directions

1. Preheat the oven to 350 degrees F.
2. In a large bowl, add all ingredients and mix until well blended.
3. Make balls from coconut mixture.
4. Place he balls on cookie sheet.
5. Bake for about 11 to 12 minutes.
6. Serve these macaroons with the dusting of gluten free cocoa powder

Quick Fruit Pudding

This is an interesting and quick dessert recipe which will result in a soft ice cream consistency from the frozen cherries. Add a little natural stevia if you crave for a sweeter taste.

Serves: *4*
Prep Time: *5 minutes*

½ cup almond milk
2 avocadoes, pitted
3 cups frozen cherries, pitted

Directions

1. In a blender, add all ingredients.
2. Blend until a creamy and smooth puree forms.
3. Serve this pudding with the topping of maraschino cherries.

Orange Blueberry Compote

This is a simple compote recipe for you to prepare a great dessert for family or friends. This luscious compote will complement your meal well.

Serves: *4*
Prep Time: *10 minutes*
Cooking Time: *5 minutes plus refrigeration time*

1¼ cups water
1¾ cups of fresh blueberries
¼ cup natural stevia (or to taste)
½ cup plus 2 tablespoons fresh orange juice
1 teaspoon orange zest, grated freshly
¼ teaspoon cinnamon powder
½ teaspoon gluten-free vanilla extract
3 large oranges, peeled, seeded and separated the segments

Directions

1. In a pan, add water, blueberries, stevia, ½ cup of orange juice, zest, cinnamon and vanilla and bring to a boil on medium-high heat.
2. Cook, stirring occasionally for about 4 to 5 minutes.
3. Remove from heat and transfer into a serving bowl.
4. Cover and refrigerate to chill.
5. Add orange segments and remaining juice in blueberry mixture and serve.
6. Serve this compote with the garnishing of fresh mint leaves.

Chocolaty Almond Truffles

These truffles feature almond and chocolate for a decadent sweet treat. Enjoy this healthy treat after dinner or as a snack at snack time.

Serves: 4
Prep Time: 10 minutes
Cooking Time: 2-4 minutes plus 1 hour refrigeration

6-ounces 70% cocoa organic chocolate, chopped finely
Pinch of cinnamon powder
Pinch of flaked sea salt
1/4 cup dried cranberries
6 tablespoons organic coconut milk
½ cup almonds, chopped

Directions

1. In a bowl, place chopped chocolate and keep aside.
2. In a pan, add cinnamon, salt and milk on medium heat.
3. Bring to a simmer.
4. Pour hot milk over chopped chocolate and stir well.
5. Cover and refrigerate for about 1 hour.
6. Place chopped almonds in a plate.
7. Make small balls from cranberry mixture.
8. Roll the balls in chopped almonds.
9. Sprinkle gluten-free cocoa powder before serving.

Simple Berry Mixed Fruit Salad

This mixed fruit salad is a yummy dessert that can be prepared in very little time. Remember that this meal should be used in moderation due to the sweetness of the ripe banana and other fruits.

Serves: *4*
Prep Time: *15 minutes*

¼ *cup blackberries*
¼ *cup raspberries*
¼ *cup strawberries, hulled and sliced*
1 small apple, peeled, cored and chopped
1 small pear, peeled, cored and chopped
2 teaspoon fresh lemon juice

Directions

1. In a large bowl, add all ingredients.
2. Gently, toss to coat well.
3. Cover and refrigerate to chill.
4. Sprinkle this fruity salad with chopped walnuts.

Banana Co-Co Rolls

These coconut coated bananas are a special and delicious treat for the whole family. This dessert must be consumed with moderation due to the sweetness of the bananas or feel free to make your own substitutions.

Serves: *2*
Prep Time: *10 minutes*

---

4 teaspoons unsweetened coconut, shredded and toasted
4 teaspoons gluten-free cocoa powder
2 ripe bananas, peeled and sliced

Directions

1. In 2 plates, place cocoa powder and shredded coconut.
2. Roll sliced bananas in cocoa powder.
3. Then roll into shredded coconut and serve.

Nutty Orange Treat

This simple fruity treat is a refreshing way to end a meal. The oranges add a tangy touch to this dessert. This dessert must be consumed with moderation due to the sweetness of the dates or feel free to make your own substitutions.

Serves: *4*
Prep Time: *10 minutes*

---

6 oranges, peeled, seeded and sectioned
2-3 dates, pitted and chopped
¼ cup walnuts, toasted and chopped
¼ teaspoon cinnamon powder
¼ teaspoon fresh lime rind, grated freshly
½ tablespoon fresh lime juice

Directions

1. In a bowl, add all ingredients and mix well.
2. Refrigerate to chill for about 30 minutes.

Spiced Pumpkin Pie

This pie is made without a crust which saves on calories and fats. Surely family and friends will enjoy this yummy pumpkin pie.

Serves: *4*
Prep Time: *10 minutes*
Cooking Time: *50 minutes*

---

2 teaspoons natural stevia
2 free-range eggs, beaten
Flaked sea salt, to taste
Pinch of ginger powder
¼ teaspoon nutmeg powder
¼ teaspoon cardamom powder
¼ teaspoon clove powder
15-ounce (a little under 2 cups) pumpkin puree
1¼ cups unsweetened almond milk
¼ cup pecans, chopped

Directions

1. Preheat the oven to 400 degrees F.
2. Lightly grease a pie dish.
3. In a large bowl, add stevia, eggs, salt and spices and mix well.
4. Stir in pumpkin puree and milk.
5. Place the pumpkin mixture in a pie dish.
6. Sprinkle pecans on top evenly.
7. Bake for 15 minutes.
8. Reduce the heat of oven to 350 degrees F.

9. Bake for 30 to 35 minutes more.

powder and spices and mix well.

3. In another bowl, add remaining ingredients and beat until well combined.
4. Mix pumpkin puree mixture into flour mixture.
5. Place the mixture in prepared muffin tray.
6. Bake for 18 to 20 minutes or until a toothpick inserted in the center comes out clean.
7. Serve these muffins with fresh fruit.

SMOOTHIES

Creamy Kale Splash Smoothie

This creamy kale smoothie is loaded with antioxidants plus essential vitamins and minerals. This is considered a low sugar smoothie which has sugar mainly from the blueberries and banana.

Serves: *2*
Prep Time: *10 minutes*

---

1 cup water
1 cup kale, washed and torn
½ of an avocado
½ cup blueberries, fresh
½ of a very ripe banana
½ cup ice cubes

Directions

Place the water in the blender first then add in the remaining ingredients. Blend until you achieve your desired smoothie consistency. In order to adjust the consistency, add more water if necessary.

Gingery Spinach Smoothie

By using spinach in this smoothie, it will give a very nice consistency and powerful nutrients when combined with the other ingredients.

***Serves:** 2*
***Prep Time:** 10 minutes*

---

1 cup strawberries, fresh
1 cup spinach, washed and torn
½ cup water (add more to adjust consistency)
1 tablespoon lemon or lime juice
2 teaspoons ginger, freshly peeled and grated
1 cup ice cubes

Directions:

Place the water in the blender first then add in the remaining ingredients. Blend until you achieve your desired smoothie consistency. In order to adjust the consistency, add more water if necessary.

Blackberry Pecan Smoothie

This smoothie uses a healthy combination of fresh blackberries which are loaded with essential vitamins, minerals and fiber. It also uses pecan butter which has healthy fat and isn't very sweet.

Serves: 2
Prep Time: 10 minutes

---

1 cup fresh blackberries (you may substitute with your favorite berries)
4 tablespoons almond milk
2 tablespoons natural smooth pecan butter
2 teaspoons natural stevia (optional)
1 cup ice cubes

Directions

Place the almond milk in the blender first then add in the remaining ingredients. Blend until you achieve your desired smoothie consistency. In order to adjust the consistency, add more almond milk if necessary.

Raspberry Bliss Smoothie

Raspberry Bliss smoothie is rich in antioxidants, healthy fats and fiber. It has no sugar added except for that which comes from the raspberries and is great for satisfying hunger pangs.

Serves: *1-2*
Prep Time: *10 minutes*

---

1 cup water
1 cup fresh raspberries
½ ripe avocado
½ cup pak choi
1 cup ice cubes

Directions

Place all ingredients into your blender and process until a smooth consistency is achieved or for about a minute. Pour in a glass and serve.

Cocoa Spiced Berry Smoothie

This brainy spiced smoothie is packed with vitamins and minerals. It has the benefits of cinnamon in it which is great for lowering cholesterol and blood sugar levels.

Serves: 2
Prep Time: 10 minutes

1½ cups fresh berries
½ very ripe banana
½ cup unsweetened organic almond milk
2 tablespoon unsweetened cocoa powder
2 teaspoon cinnamon extract
¾ cup water
½ cup ice cubes

Directions

Place all ingredients into your blender and process until smooth consistency is achieved or for about a minute. Pour in a glass and serve.

Avocado Almond Smoothie

This healthy low carb smoothie is a great almond treat which is made very creamy with a slice of avocado. Drink this healthy glass of smoothie and boost your energy levels.

Serves: *1*
Prep Time: *10 minutes*

---

1 cup unsweetened almond milk
1 slice ripe avocado
2 tablespoons natural almond butter
1 tablespoon cacao powder
1 tablespoon natural stevia
¼ cup ice cubes

Directions

Place all ingredients into your blender and process until smooth or for about a minute. Pour in a glass and serve.

Cucumber Breeze Smoothie

This smoothie recipe is great for the skin and kidneys. Drink to your brain's health while also enjoying every sip of this fiber-rich smoothie.

Serves: 2
Prep Time: 10 minutes

---

2 large cucumbers, washed, peeled and cut into chunks
1 cup unsweetened almond milk
1 cup frozen raspberries (ensure that these are free from added sugar)
1 tablespoon natural stevia
1 teaspoon vanilla extract
1 teaspoon lemon juice

Directions

Place all ingredients into your blender and process until smooth consistency is achieved or for about a minute. Pour in a glass and serve.

Green Brain Tonic Smoothie

This is an extremely healthy smoothie for the brain and it has no added sugar except for these low sugar fruits. It is loaded with essential vitamins and minerals to boost your brain power and enhance your overall health. You'll know you're drinking something healthy with every sip.

Serves: *2*
Prep Time: *10 minutes*

---

1 large handful of kale or spinach
½ of a bell pepper
¾ of an avocado
2 cloves garlic
2 ripe tomatoes
2 cups of water

Directions

Place all ingredients into your blender and process until smooth consistency is achieved or for about a minute. Pour in a glass and serve.

7-DAY GLUTEN-FREE MEAL PLAN

Here follows a 7-Day Gluten-free meal plan to help you to hit the ground running. Please make necessary adjustments to the recipe proportions based on the required servings.

Bear in mind that some meals may require prior preparation; hence, in order to make the necessary preparations, it is necessary to review the menu recipes prior to the actual day of preparation.

*Note that the meals that are in **bold** can be found in this cookbook.*

~ DAY 1 ~

Today is a protein-rich day, accompanied by healthy nuts as a snack.

BREAKFAST: pg 17
Cheesy Pepper Baked Eggs (serve along with avocado slices)
Beverage: unsweetened organic almond milk (optional)

SNACK:
A handful of your favorite nuts: almonds, pecans or walnut

LUNCH: pg 82
Zucchini Lasagna with Chicken & Ricotta

DINNER:
99   41
Spicy Salmon Stew with **Baby Spinach Olive Salad**
Dessert: **Chocolaty Almond Truffles**

137

~ DAY 2 ~

Today, it's a very healthy brain menu. Enjoy every bite.

BREAKFAST:
69

Spinach & Green Peppers Omelet

SNACK:

Carrot cut into long bite-size strips) dipped in Pecan Nut Butter

LUNCH:
154

Green Brain Tonic Smoothie

DINNER:
113

Lamb Chops with Roasted Cherry Tomatoes
Dessert: **Orange Cashew Pudding** (leave leftover for next day)

143

~ DAY 3 ~

It's a very comforting menu today.

BREAKFAST: 23
Veggie Breakfast Scramble

SNACK:
An apple or a few of your favorite nuts

LUNCH:
Herbed Tomato Soup 48

DINNER: 15
Herbed Cheesy Chicken Wings with fresh greens
Dessert: leftover **Orange Cashew Pudding** from previous day
143

~ DAY 4 ~

Enjoy today's fish & seafood day plus vegetables for your sides if you wish.

BREAKFAST: *13*
Mini Kale & Mushrooms Quiches

SNACK:
¼ cup shredded coconut topped with a sprinkle of natural stevia

90 LUNCH: *98*
Wild Salmon with Arugula Pesto Salad or Grilled Shrimp with Herbs

DINNER: *94*
Black Cod with Artichokes & Lemon
Dessert: 3 dark chocolate squares (ensure that chocolate has 70% or more cocoa)

~ DAY 5 ~

Today is your "go dairy-free" day! Going dairy-free never tasted so good.

BREAKFAST:
Poached or boiled eggs and avocado slices

SNACK:
½ cup of your favorite berries

LUNCH: 56
Stir Fry Baby Bok Choy & Bell Pepper

DINNER: 79
Roasted Chicken Drumsticks with Fennel
Dessert: **A Pumpkin & Coconut Muffin** (leave leftover for the following day) 144

~ DAY 6 ~

This is your meatless day. Enjoy your meat-free meals.

BREAKFAST: *15*
Mushroom Artichoke Frittata

SNACK:
A handful of your favorite nuts

LUNCH:
Olive Grilled Asparagus *63*

DINNER: *64*
Baked Cheesy Summer Squash
Dessert: A leftover **Pumpkin & Coconut Muffin** from the
previous day. *144*

~ DAY 7 ~

*Get a full gluten-free variety today. A little variety always takes care of
any hint of boredom.*

BREAKFAST:
Crustless Mushroom Quiche 32

SNACK:
Cucumber slices sprinkles with a little sea salt and pepper or
dipped in plain yogurt

LUNCH: 101
Cherry Roasted Wild Herring

DINNER: 117
Spiced Ground Beef & Zucchini
Dessert: **Simple Berry Mixed Fruit Salad** 138

14 FOODS LIST GUIDE

Here is a helpful guide of typical brain healthy and gluten-free for your shopping list.

1. **Healthy Wild Fish** such as: blue crab, sardines, shrimp, flounder, anchovies, sole, wild salmon and herring
2. **Non-starchy Vegetables** such as: cabbage, turnip, bok choy, broccoli, lettuce, mushroom, squash, cauliflower, cucumber, tomatoes, bell peppers, celery, onions, zucchini and green leafy vegetables such as: kale, spinach, mixed greens.
3. **Healthy Nuts** such as: almonds, walnuts, pecans
4. **Healthy Seeds** such as: chia seeds, flaxseeds, pumpkin seeds, sunflower seeds, sesame seeds
5. **Healthy Fats** such as: extra-virgin olive oil and coconut oil, grass-fed butter, ghee, avocado, shredded coconut
6. **Healthy Proteins** such as: grass-fed beef, organic pork, free-range chicken and turkey, free-range eggs
7. **Healthy Sugars** such as: low sugar fruits including limes, pumpkin, lemons, natural stevia, berries, cantaloupe
8. **Healthy Vinegars**: balsamic vinegar, raw coconut vinegar, apple cider vinegar
9. **Healthy Starches**: arrowroot powder, coconut flour, almond flour, flax flour

10. **Healthy Cheeses**: most cheeses can be eaten; however, cheeses that contain gluten such as blue cheeses should be avoided.
11. **Healthy Condiments**: Avoid processed condiments such as ketchup or catsup and stick to homemade, gluten-free and low-sugar condiments instead.
12. **Healthy Beverages** such as: filtered water, organic unsweetened coconut water, organic unsweetened almond milk.
13. **Natural and Organic Herbs, Seasonings and Spices**
14. **Salt**: Flaked sea salt, coarse sea salt or regular sea salt

Bear in mind that this is not a conclusive list and simply represents food items on a typical gluten-free shopping list.

YOU CAN DO THIS!

No longer will you have to be an experienced chef or a student of food science to master the art of cooking gluten-free and brain friendly recipes. With this book's simple principles and procedures, you will know the secrets to successfully create healthy, flavorful foods that are low carb, low sugar and best of all, gluten-free.

Many people have experienced significant health improvements while living gluten-free. I am one of them! Ideally, I strongly believe that if living gluten-free improved my health, then it is quite likely that it will improve yours too. With my experience with these recipes, I can confidently say that the gluten-free lifestyle really works. I will never go back eating wheat and grains because the gluten-free health results are—*simply priceless*.

Thanks again for choosing my book. If you find this book to be helpful, I would appreciate if you would let other readers know about it by leaving a book review. I hereby wish you all the best in your quest to eat brain healthy and live a healthier life.

Yours in health,
Sheryl Jensen

Made in the USA
San Bernardino, CA
15 May 2014